THE EMPIRE STATE BUILDING

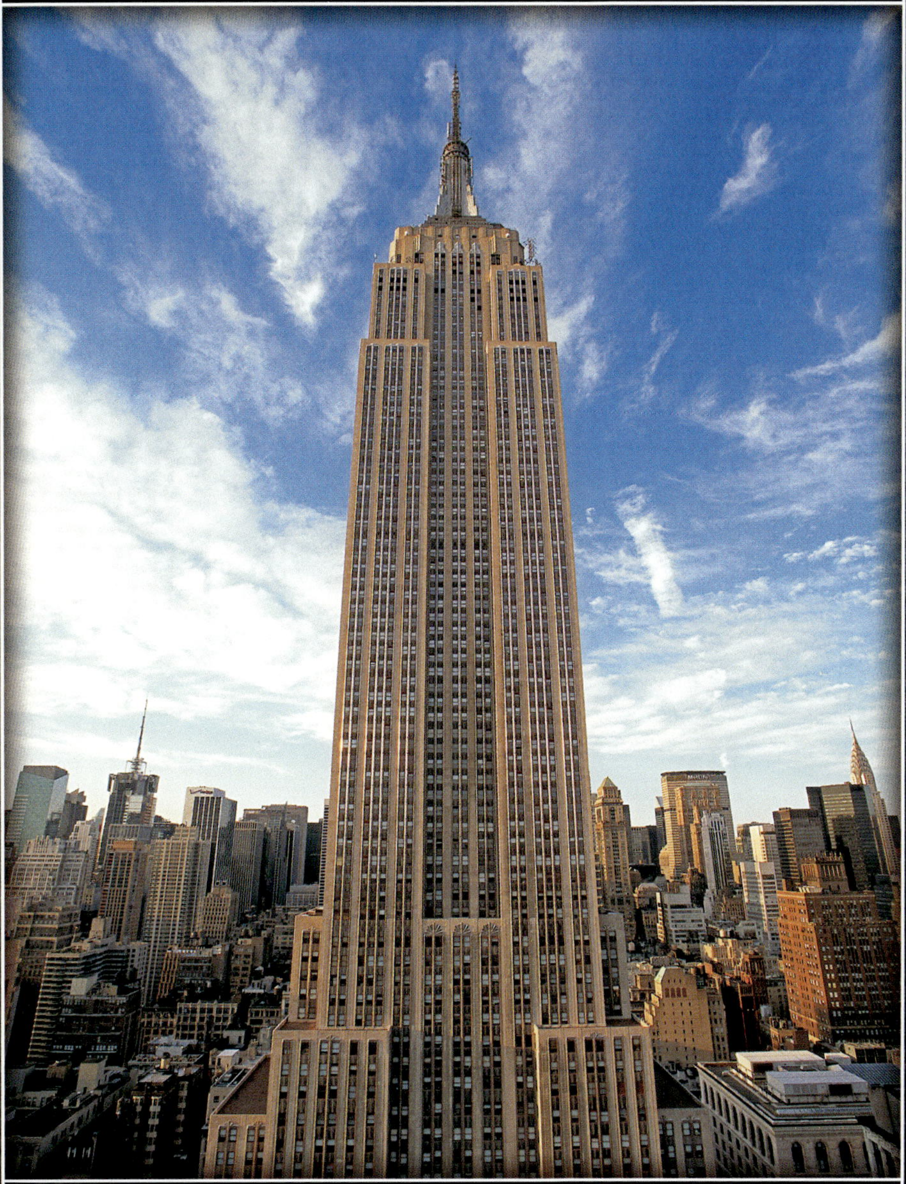

PORTRAITS OF AN AMERICAN ICON

BY JOSEPH M. LUMAN

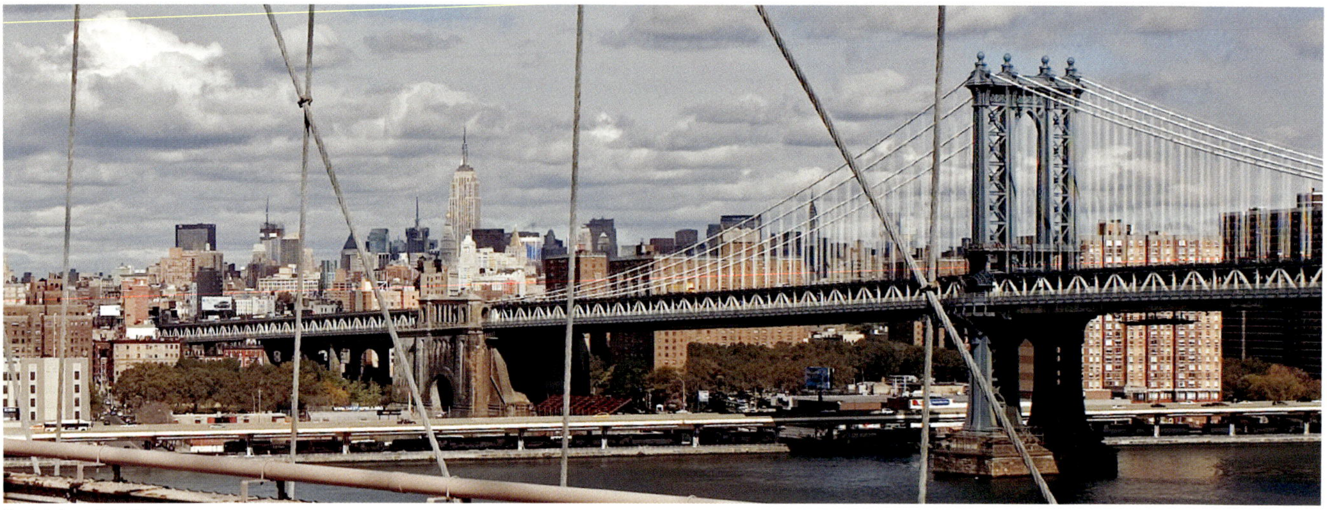

Photo by Joe Luman © Terrell Creative

THE EMPIRE STATE BUILDING: PORTRAITS OF AN AMERICAN ICON

AUTHOR & EDITOR: Joseph M. Luman

ART DIRECTION & IMAGE EDITING: Chad Combs

GRAPHIC DESIGN: Kelly Spornitz

IMAGE SELECTION & EDITORIAL SUPPORT:
Janet Rogers and Kelly Elliott

PRODUCTION: Carol Evans

PUBLISHED BY:
Designed by Terrell Creative in the USA • Printed in China

First Edition
ISBN-13: 978-1-56944-361-3
ISBN-10: 1-56944-361-0

TITLE PAGE: Photo © Richard Berenholtz

DUST JACKET: Front Cover Photo © Richard Berenholtz
Back Cover Photo by Joe Luman © Terrell Creative

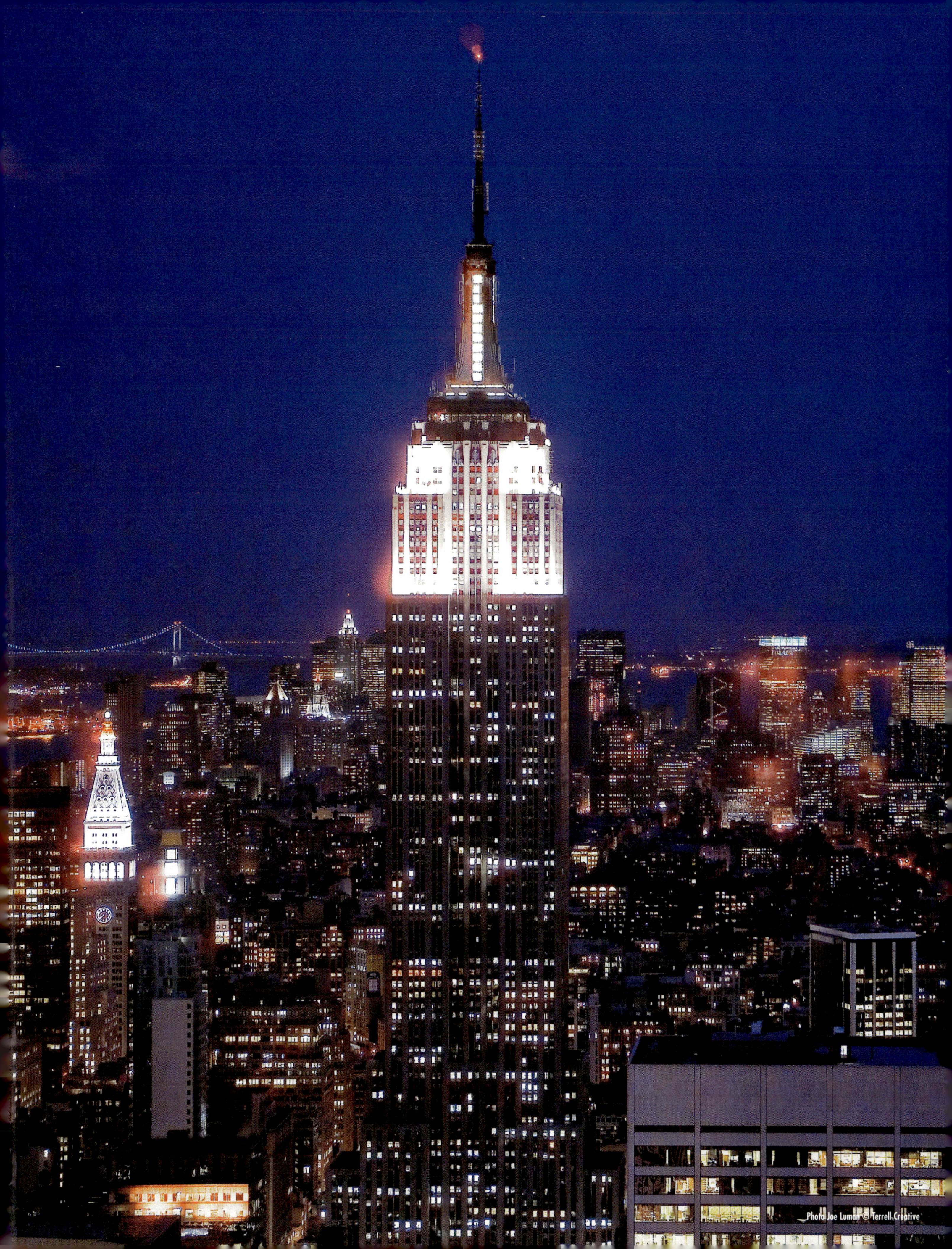

Photo Joe Luman © Terrell Creative

INTRODUCTION

For some, the Empire State Building merely conjures up visions of King Kong swatting at attacking airplanes while holding Fay Ray in one hand and hanging on to the 102nd-story tower with the other. Or, it is Tom Hanks and Meg Ryan meeting on the 86th Floor Observatory in *Sleepless in Seattle*, or Billy Crystal and Meg Ryan, same place, in *When Harry Met Sally*. For the older generation, who can forget *An Affair to Remember* with Cary Grant and Deborah Kerr?

For others, it stands as a symbol of the American "can-do" spirit. Born out of the depression, it was built with the purpose of being the tallest building in the world — a distinction that the Chrysler Building had held for a few short months. Built in less than 14 months, it is a record still held today for a building of its size. During peak periods, 3,400

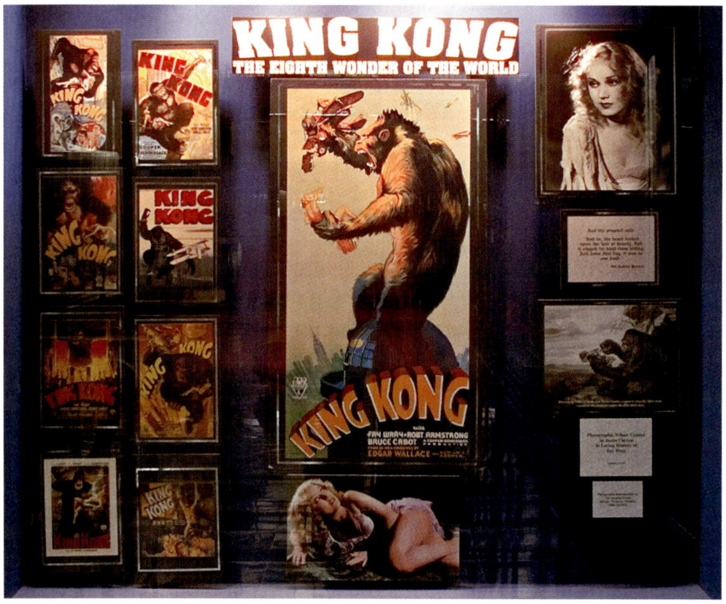

Photo by Joe Luman © Terrell Creative

people worked on the building, with 7,000,000 man hours expended to erect this grand edifice in one year and 45 days, including weekends and holidays. Five people gave their lives working on the building, and at peak production, four and a half stories were being constructed a week.

For everyone it is, again, New York City's tallest building — a reminder to those who will never forget that horrific day, September 11, 2001. It is impossible to stand on the 86th Floor Observatory, looking south toward Lower Manhattan, to the place where the Twin Towers once stood, and not think of what it would have been like for those that were there, on the observatory that fateful morning, looking out over the New York City skyline.

For me, it is a symbol of my ancestry. I am the youngest son of the only son of immigrants from Eastern Europe, who arrived at Ellis Island between 1899 and 1902. My father, Morton Luman, was born in the Bronx in 1913, graduating from PS 75, eighth grade, in 1927. A few years later came service in the CCC (Civilian Conservation Corps) and time spent out west. He met my mother while serving in the Army Air Corps when stationed for one week in Boise, Idaho. Three weeks later they were married in El Paso, Texas, and then, he was off to England to serve his country and the world. He earned the Distinguished Flying Cross for completing 25 missions over Germany as an aerial photographer. It is this photography skill that he was taught in the Army Air Corps that brings my story full circle.

As a young man I worked with my father as he photographed the Pacific Northwest, and sold his images on postcards. My love of photography has grown from this time spent with my father, and working in the tourism industry for a good portion of my life. Now, later in my life I have returned to my roots, New York City, to photograph and produce this book on the Empire State Building.

I first visited New York City and The Empire State Building when I was eight years old. My family had flown cross-country in 1960 to visit my father's stepbrother, Uncle Lew and Aunt Ruth. Even though this trip was nearly a half century ago, I still remember seeing the Empire State Building for the first time. Never before had I seen any building that could even remotely be called a skyscraper. Since that first visit, this city and its building have been etched into my soul. This is a journey back to my roots, to my memories.

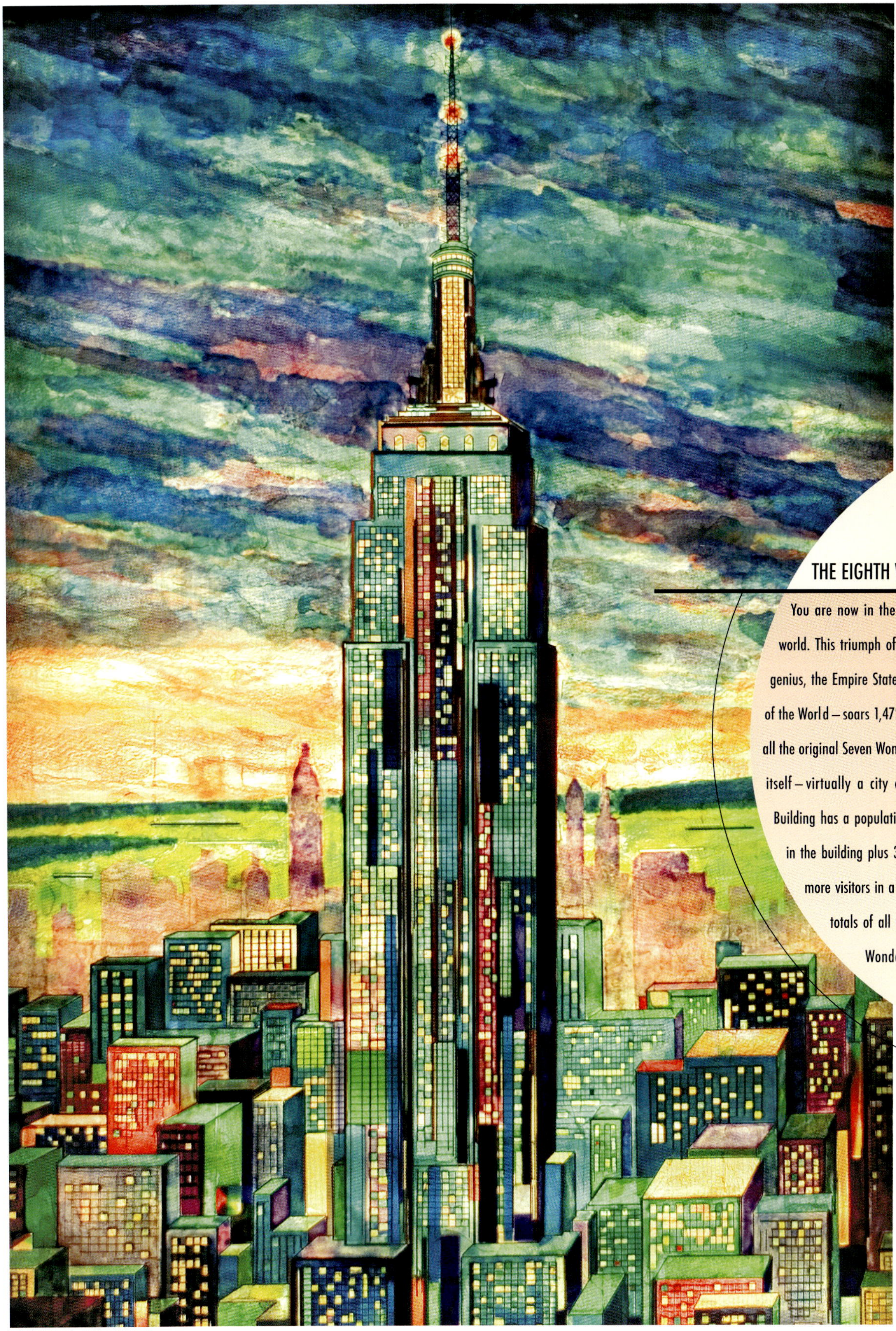

Photo by Joe Luman © Terrell Creative

THE EIGHTH WONDER OF THE WORLD

You are now in the most famous building in the world. This triumph of architectural and engineering genius, the Empire State Building– the Eighth Wonder of the World – soars 1,472 feet into the sky – as high as all the original Seven Wonders stacked together. A city in itself – virtually a city of marvel – the Empire State Building has a population of 16,000 persons working in the building plus 35,000 visitors daily – totalling more visitors in a single year than the combined totals of all who visited the original Seven Wonders of the World throughout recorded history.

BELOW: In 1930 Lewis Hine was commissioned to photograph the construction of the Empire State Building. He documented the project from the ground up and his collection stands today as one of the most poignant photo anthologies ever, documenting the relationship of man to a building. **RIGHT:** As the building nears completion the tower mast is added, making the Empire State Building the tallest building in the world.

FOLLOWING PAGES, LEFT: The Empire State Building, now completed, assumes the title of "Tallest in the World," from the Chrysler building seeming quite demure in the background. **RIGHT:** This image taken in 1937 shows the Empire State Building from lower 5th Avenue near East 17th Street.

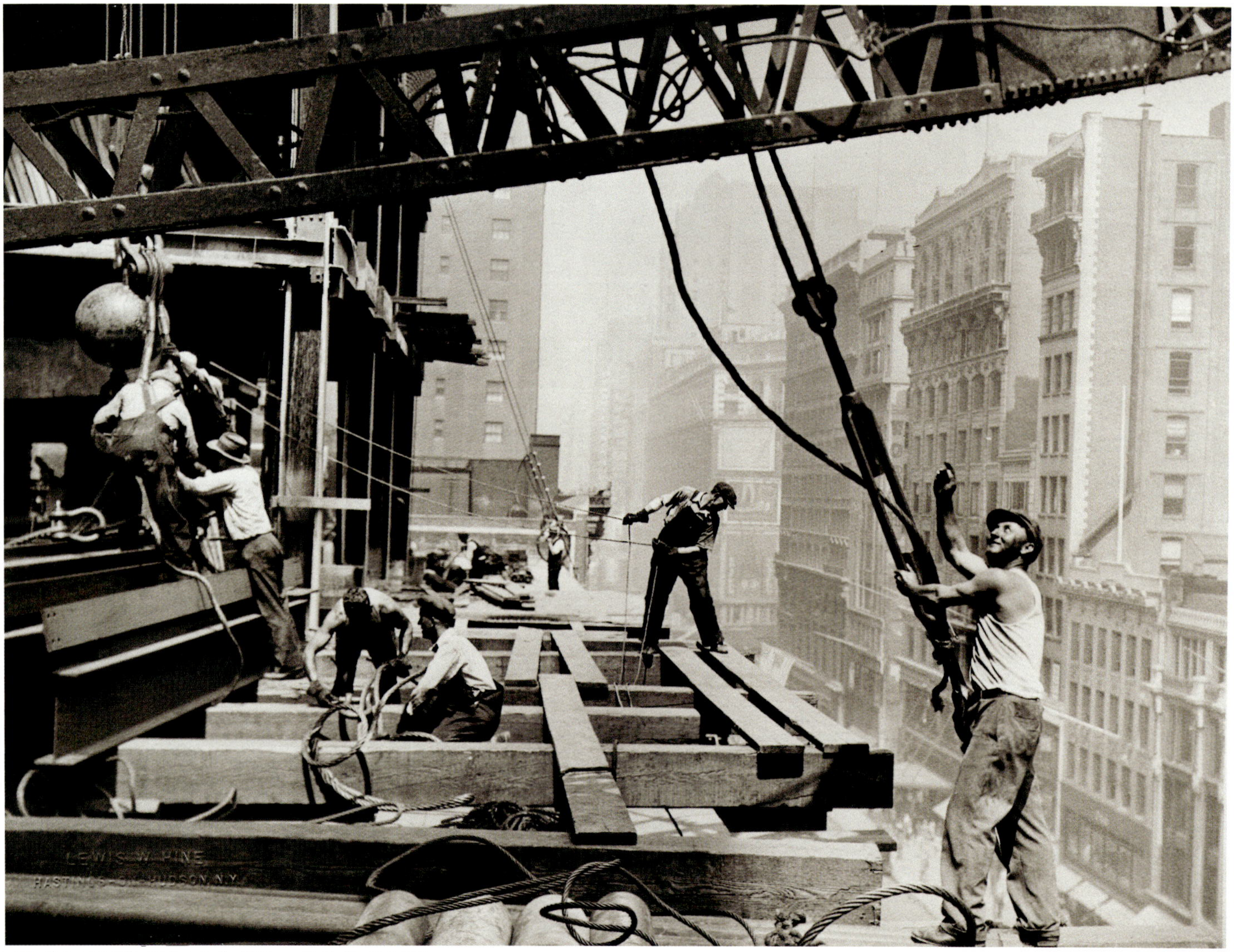

Lewis Hine, *The Empire State Building Under Construction*, Circa 1930, Museum of the City of New York (L.638.8)

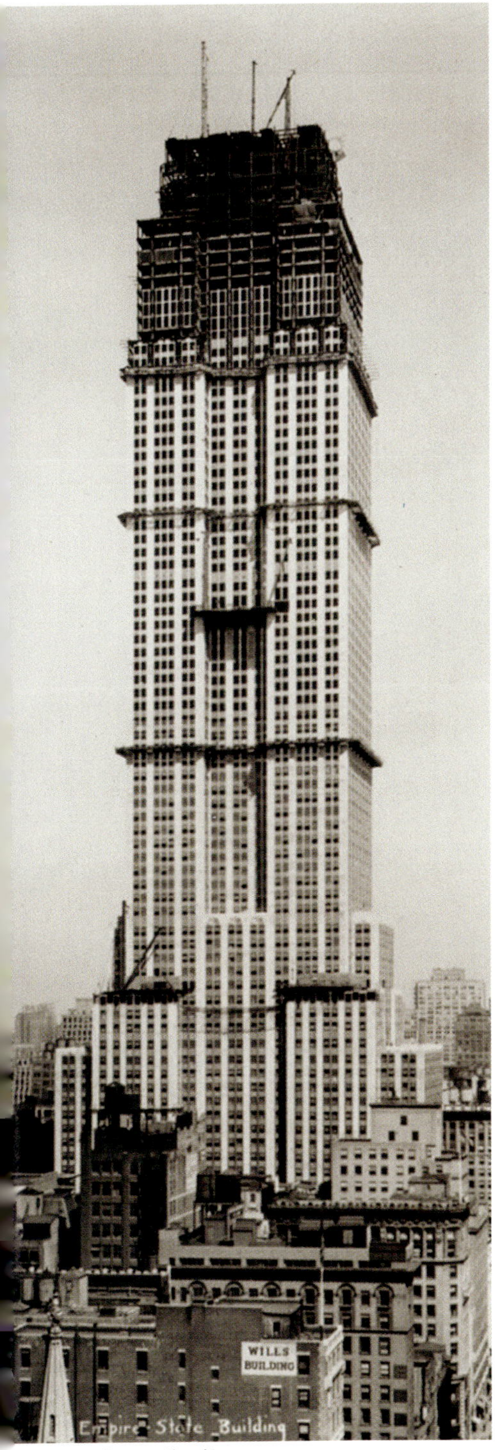

Photo courtesy Library of Congress

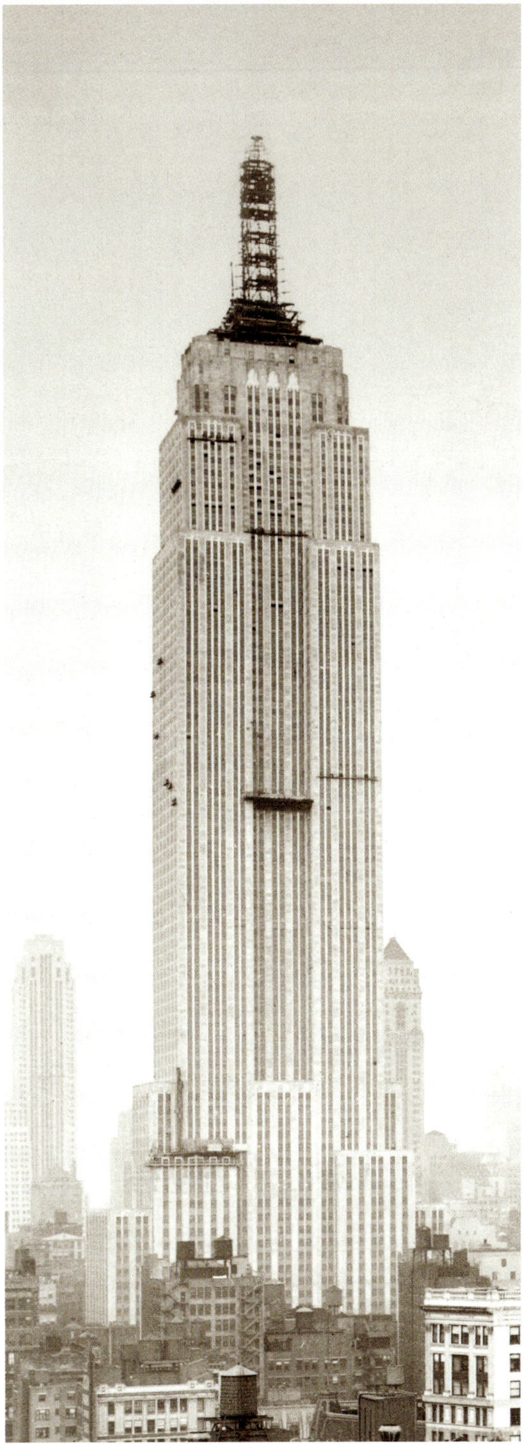
Collection of The New-York Historical Society, #72476

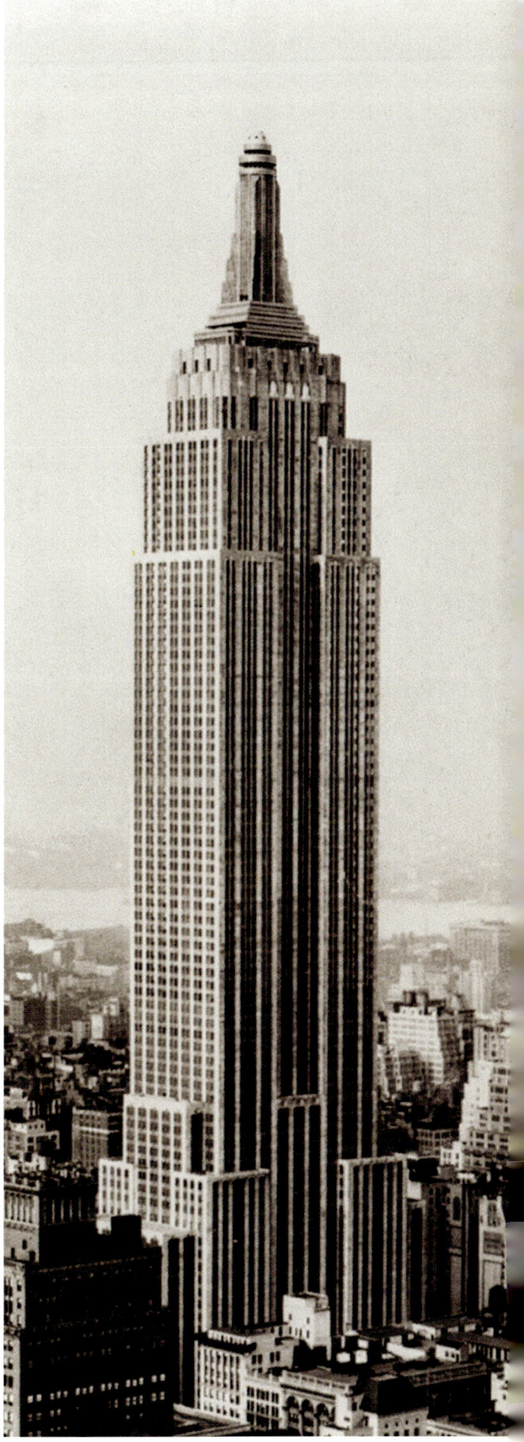
Photo courtesy Library of Congress

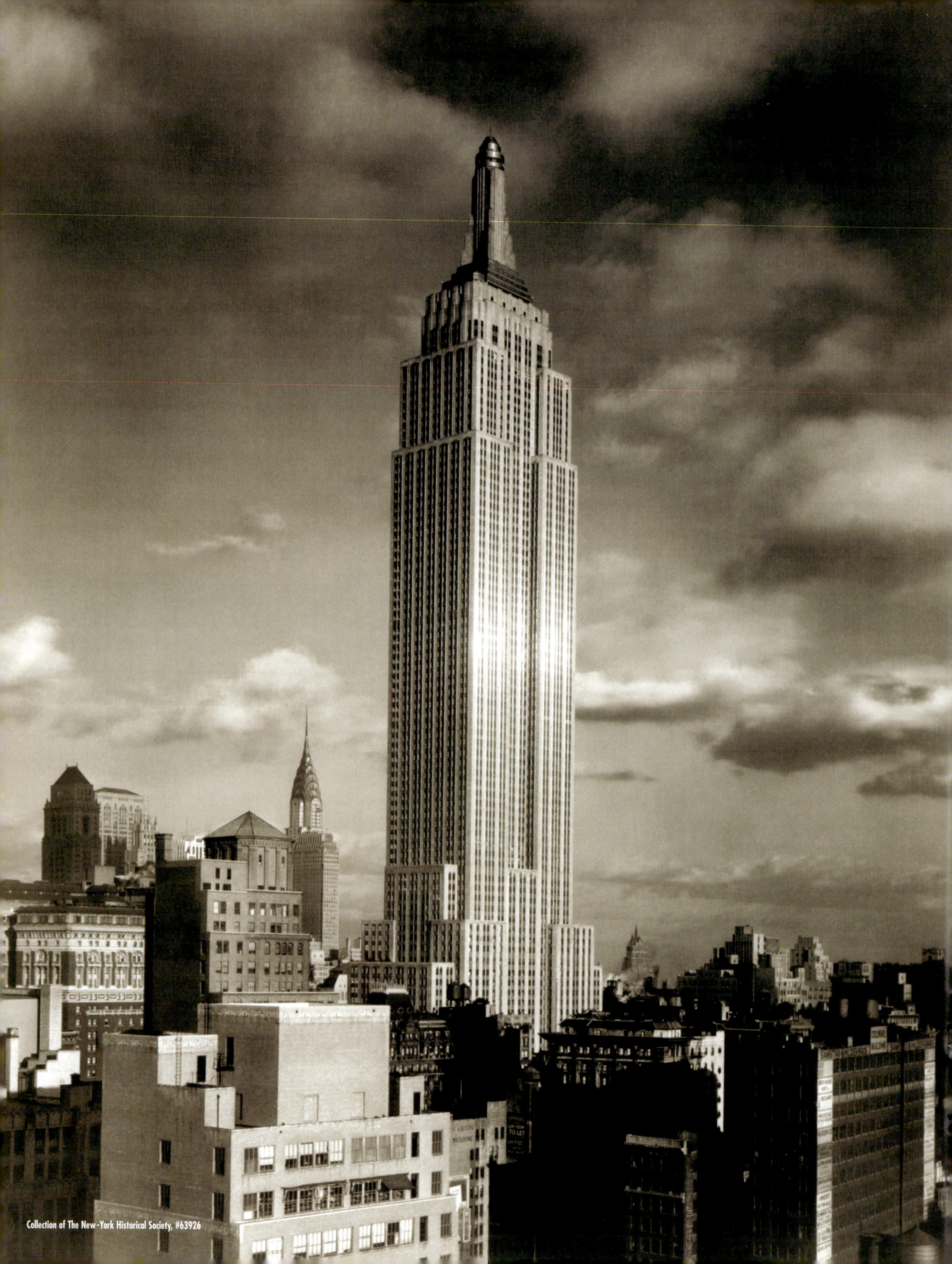

Collection of The New-York Historical Society, #63926

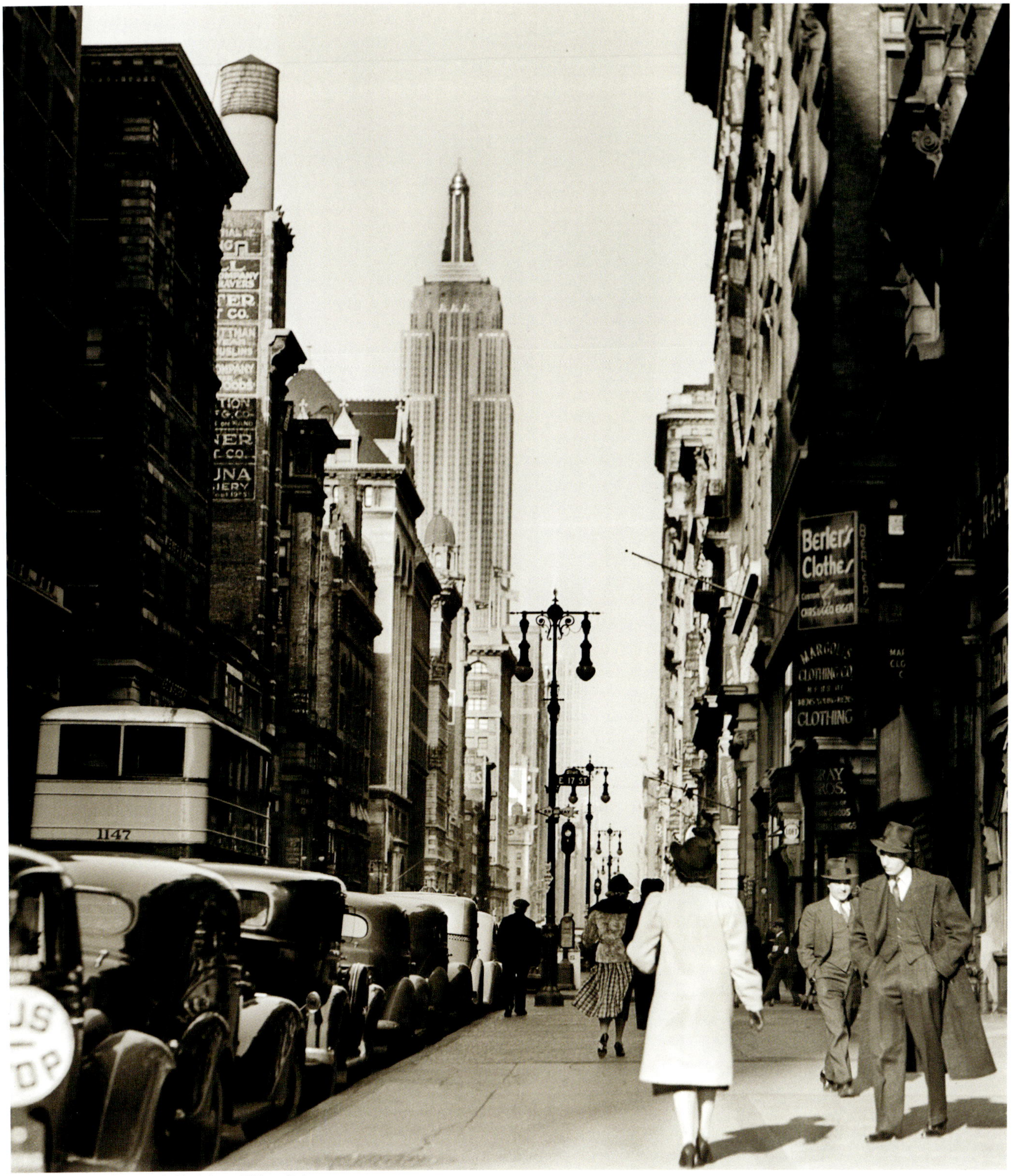

Photo #WPA 632 E. Lower Fifth Ave., 1937 by Edwards, Courtesy NYC Municipal Archives

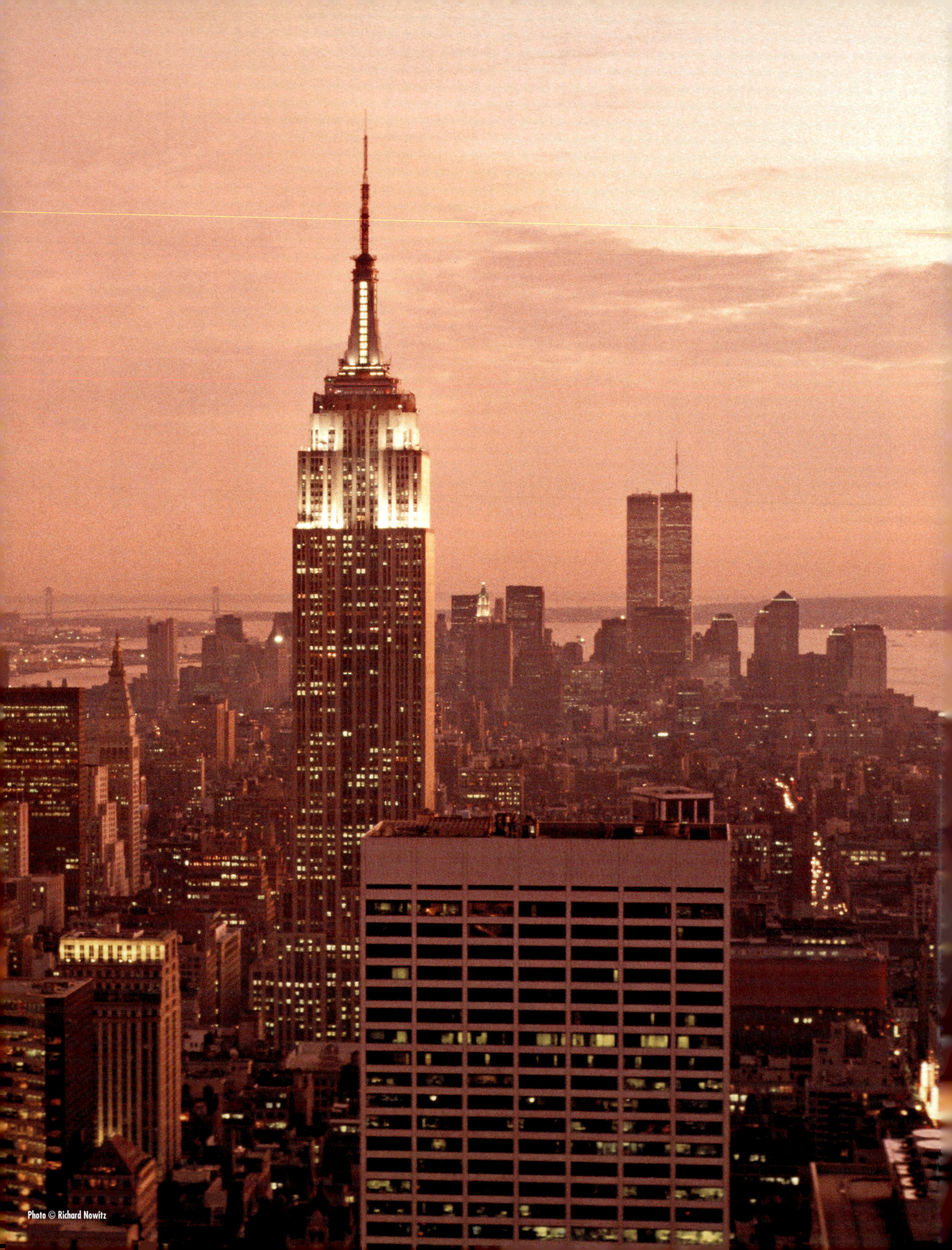

Photo © Richard Nowitz

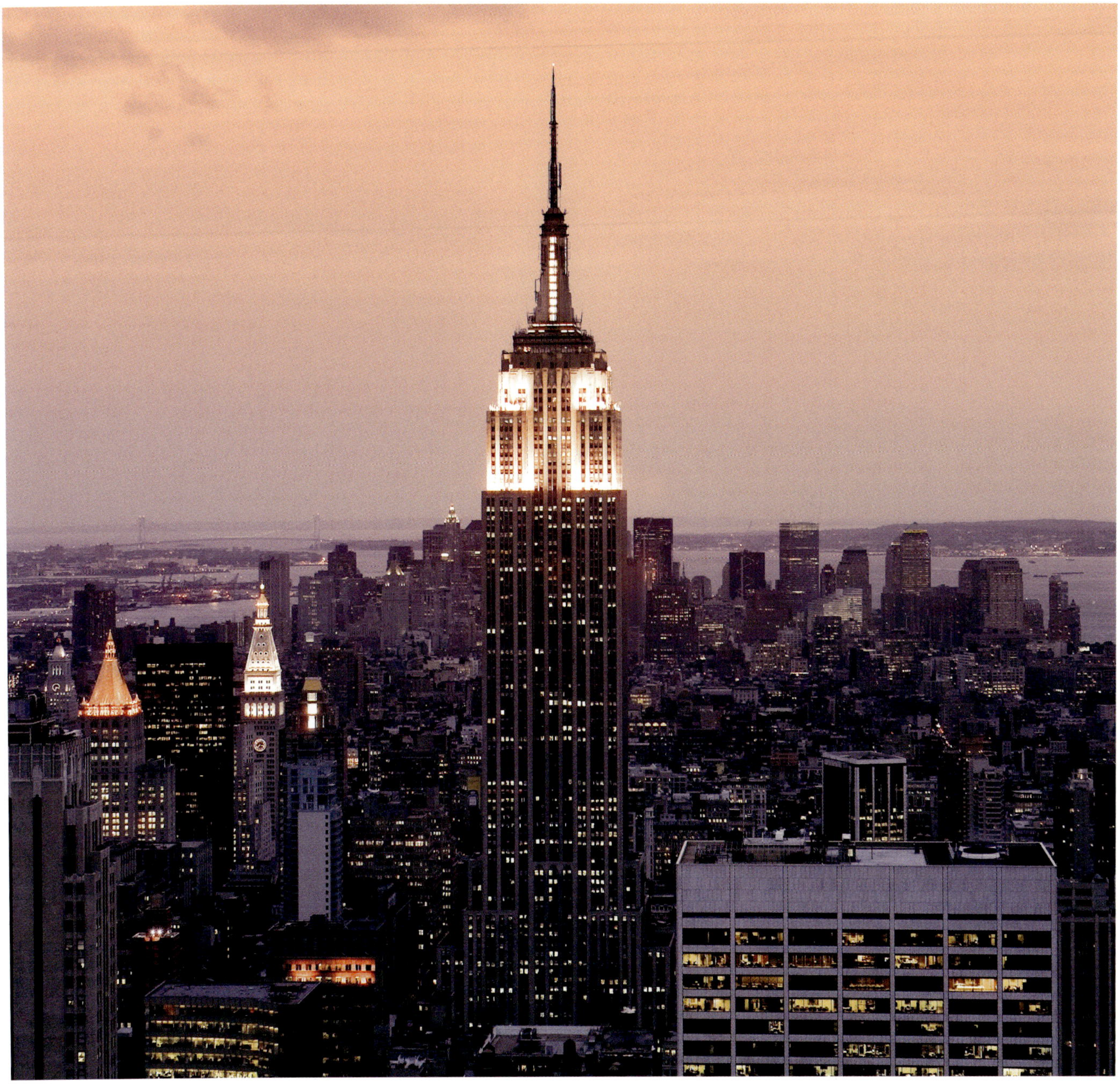

Photo by Joe Luman © Terrell Creative

LEFT: The Empire State Building lost its title of "World's Tallest Building" when the North Tower of the World Trade Center was completed in 1972. The South Tower became the second tallest building in the world when it was completed in 1973. **ABOVE:** With the tragic events of September 11, 2001, the Empire State Building again became the tallest building in New York City, but was no longer in the top five of the world. For those who had viewed the towers in the Lower Manhattan skyline for nearly 30 years, the skyline now seems incomplete in their absence.

FOLLOWING PAGES: The Empire State Building illuminated in blue/white/red was taken looking southwest towards the Hudson River and New Jersey showing the New York City skyline as it stood prior to September 11, 2001.

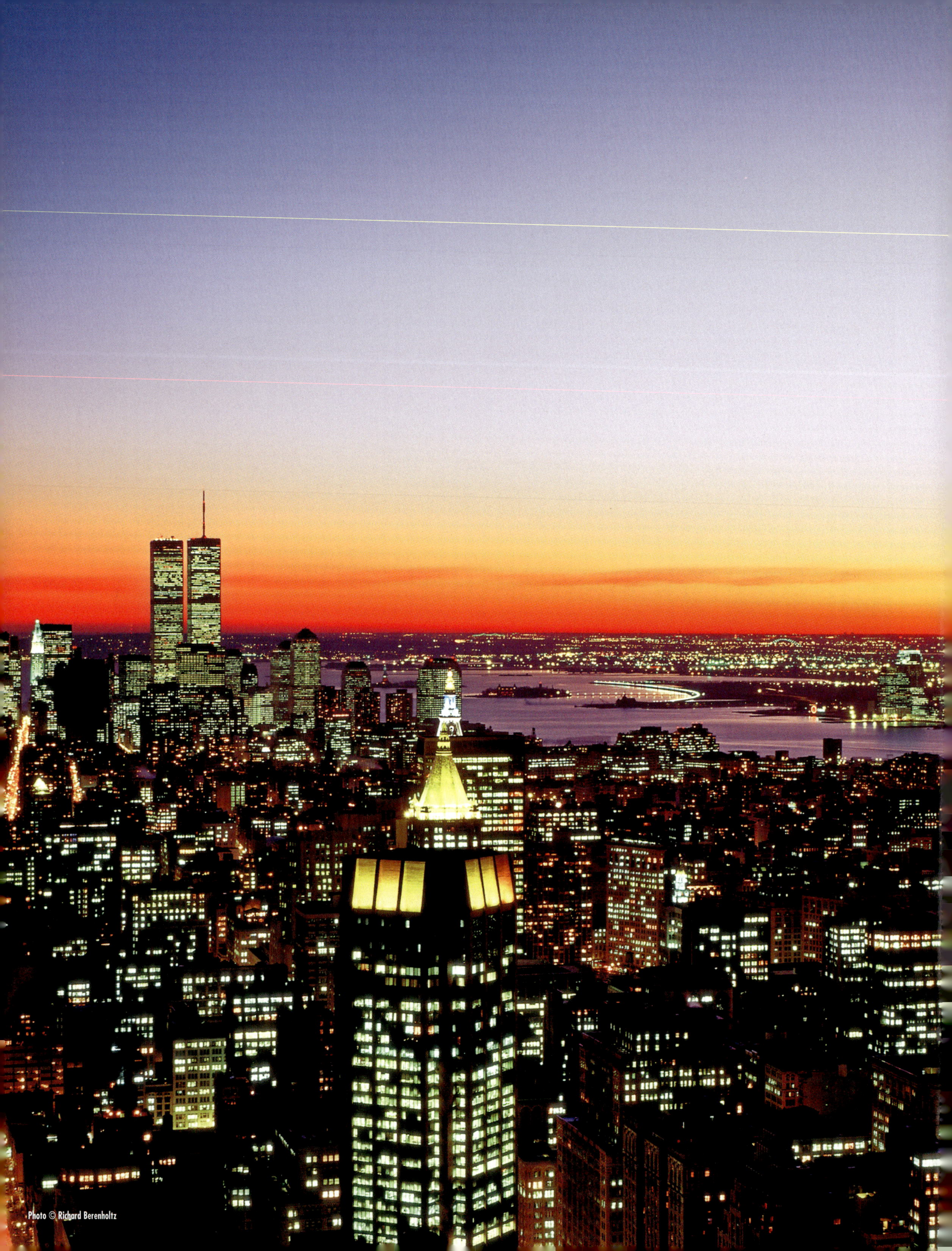

Photo © Richard Berenholtz

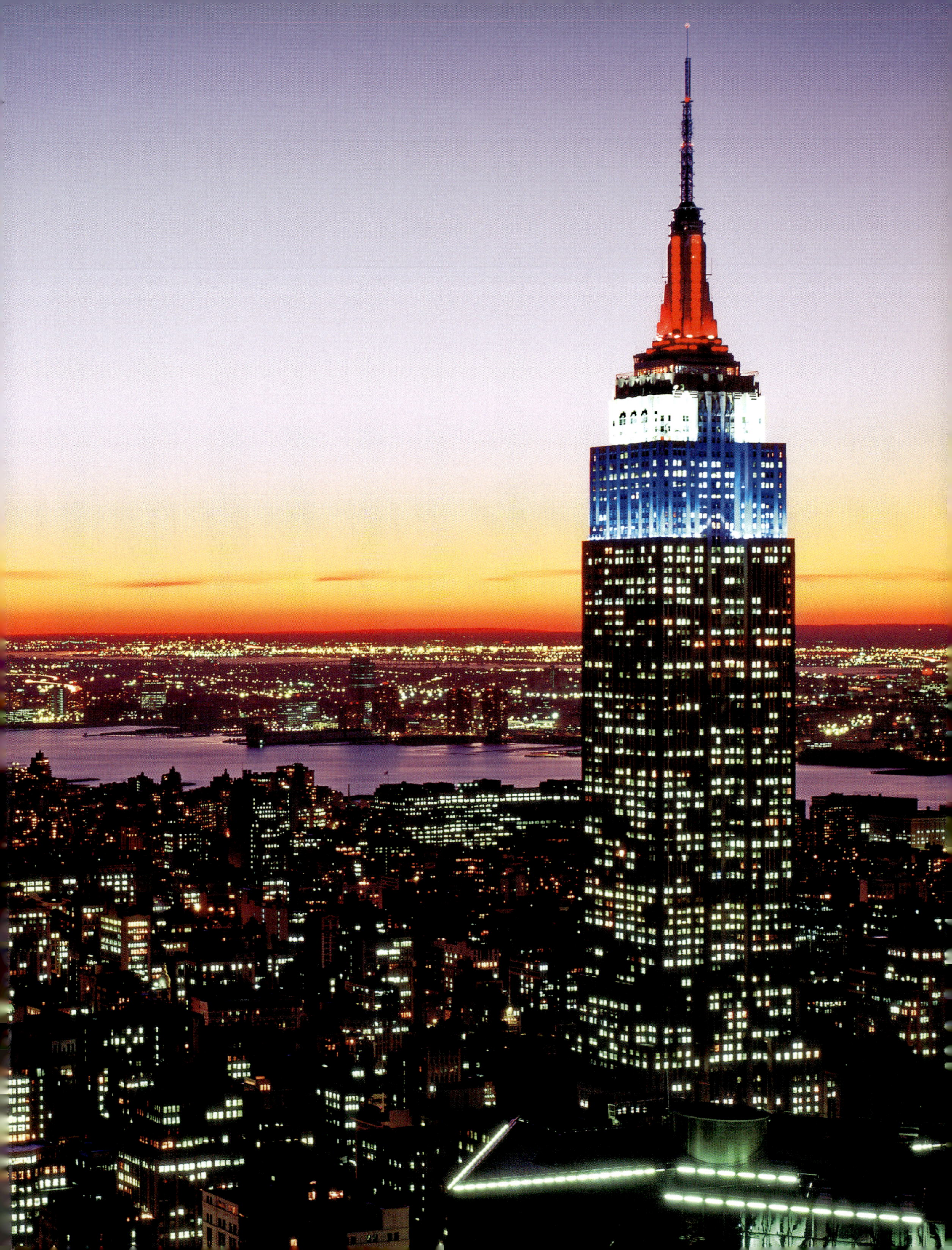

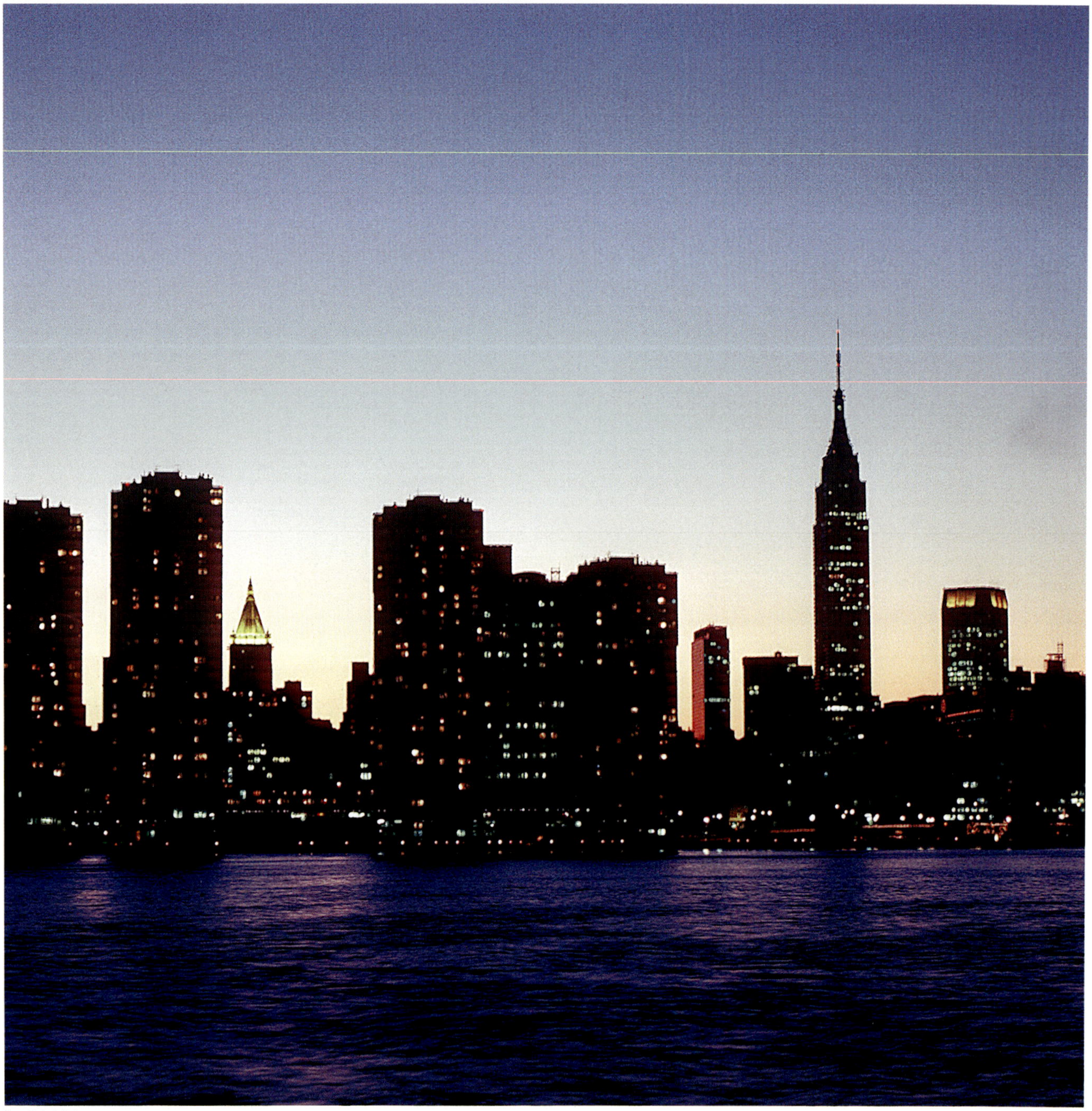

Photo © Randa Bishop

ABOVE: This vantage point, looking west from Long Island City, Queens, across the East River, allows for a breathtaking view of the Empire State Building silhouetted against the sky still illuminated after the sun has set in the west. **RIGHT:** The city awakens to a dramatic sky captured here from a building just west of the Empire State Building.

FOLLOWING PAGES: This photo depicts Midtown Manhattan as seen from across the East River. This vantage point offers a spectacular view of the Empire State Building. Notice the Chrysler Building is just peeking over the top of the United Nations Building to the right, almost looking like it is connected to and part of the United Nations Building.

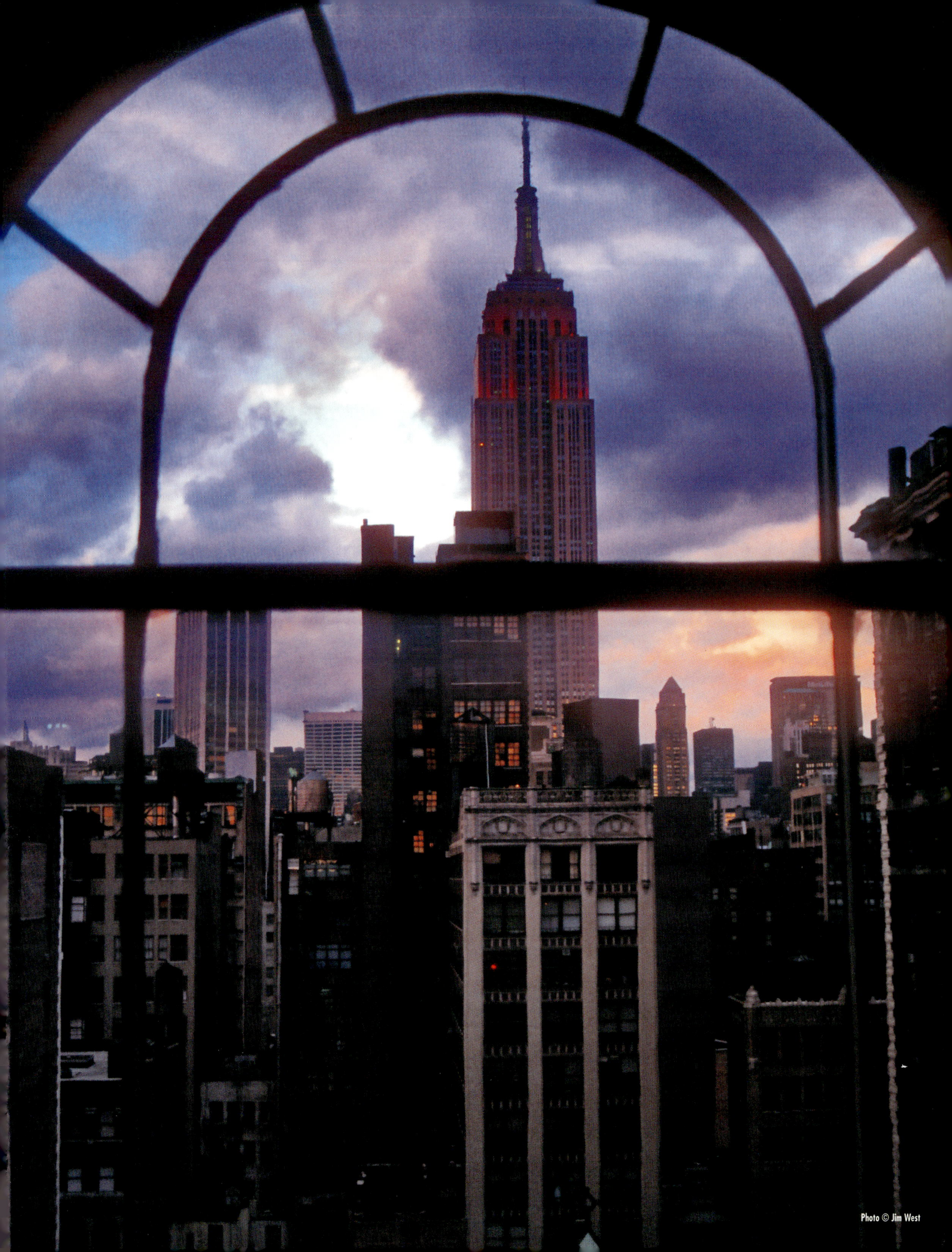
Photo © Jim West

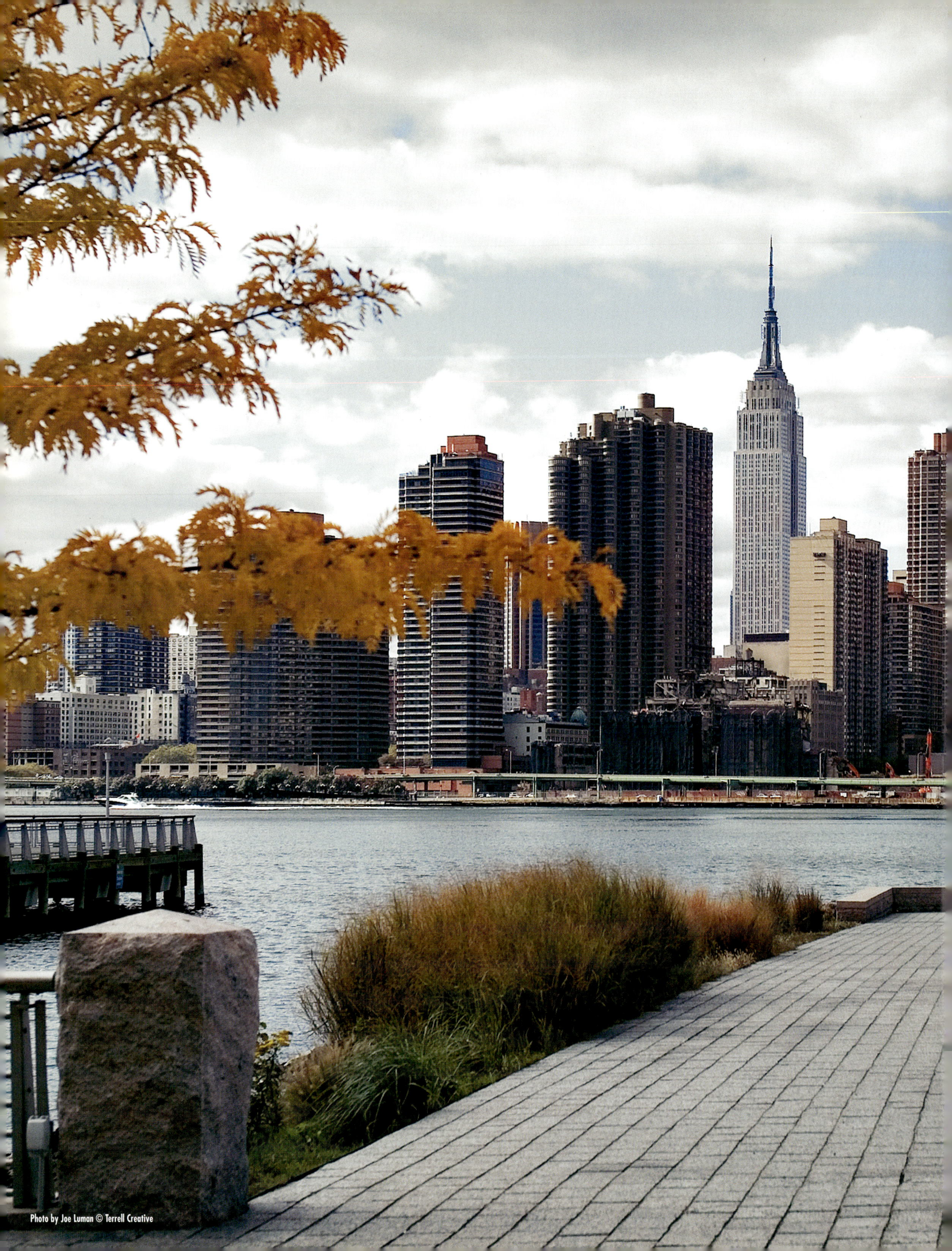

Photo by Joe Luman © Terrell Creative

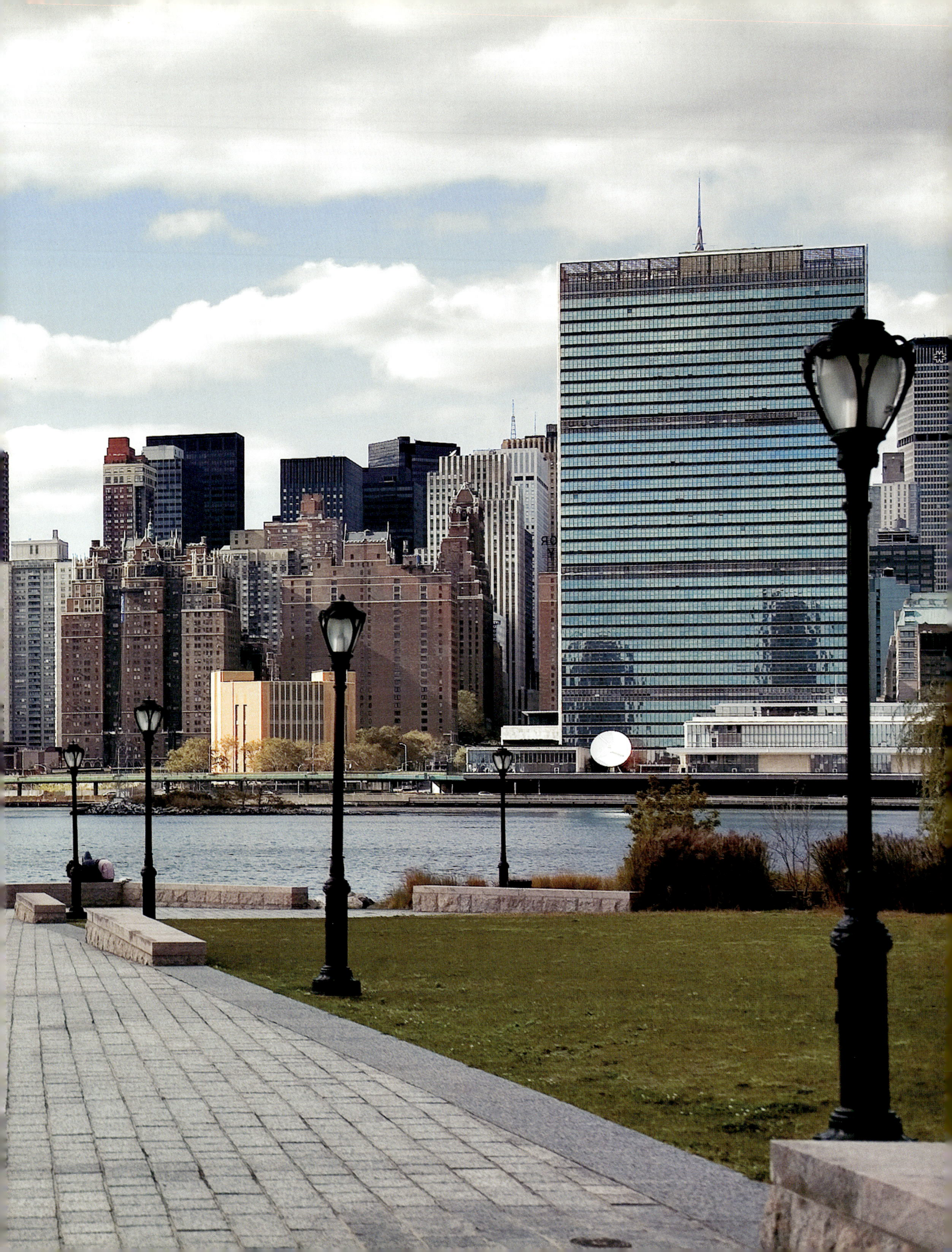

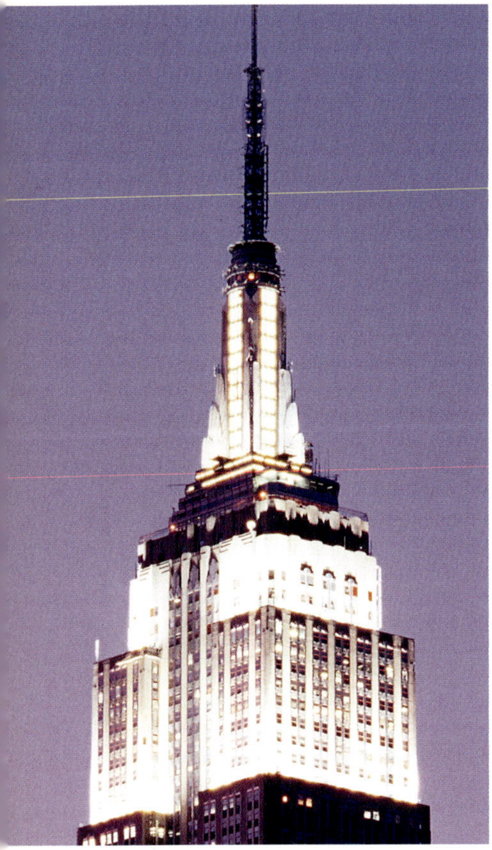
Photo © Patrick Batchelder

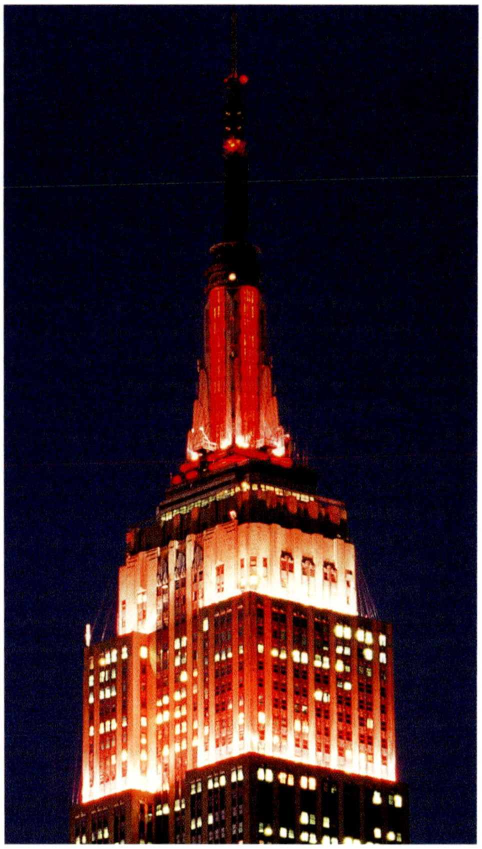
Photo © Patrick Batchelder

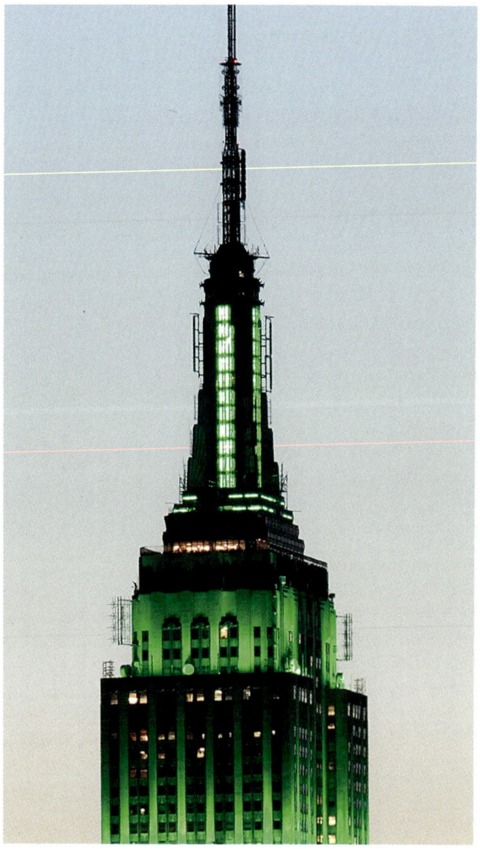
Photo © Walter Bibikow/DanitaDelimont.com

ABOVE: (from left to right) The traditional Empire State Building lighting is white/white/white, used on any day that there is no special lighting required. The red/red/red is used for Valentine's Day, as well as other special days such as GO RUTGERS! The green/green/green is used on St. Patrick's Day, and has been used to commemorate the 75th anniversary of Popeye, and Earth Day. The red/white/blue configuration is one of the most used color combinations. In addition to Independence Day, these colors are used for Memorial Day, Veterans' Day, Presidents' Day, Labor Day, Flag Day, Election Day, and others. Since September 11, 2001 the red/white/blue colors have been used to memorialize that infamous day. **RIGHT:** (from left to right) The orange/orange/blue scheme has been used for the New York City Marathon as well as the NYC 2012 Olympic campaign. The red/red/yellow is used to commemorate the anniversary of the United State Marines. It signifies autumn and also this color combination is used when the Ringling Bros./Barnum and Bailey Circus is in town. Green/white/red signifies Mexican Independence Day, and blue/white/blue signifies Hanukkah, Israel Independence Day, as well as Jackie Robinson Day.

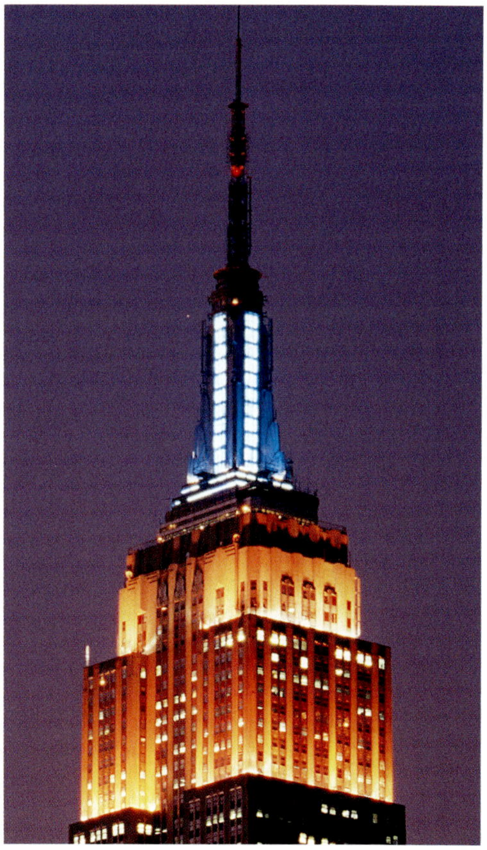
Photo © Patrick Batchelder

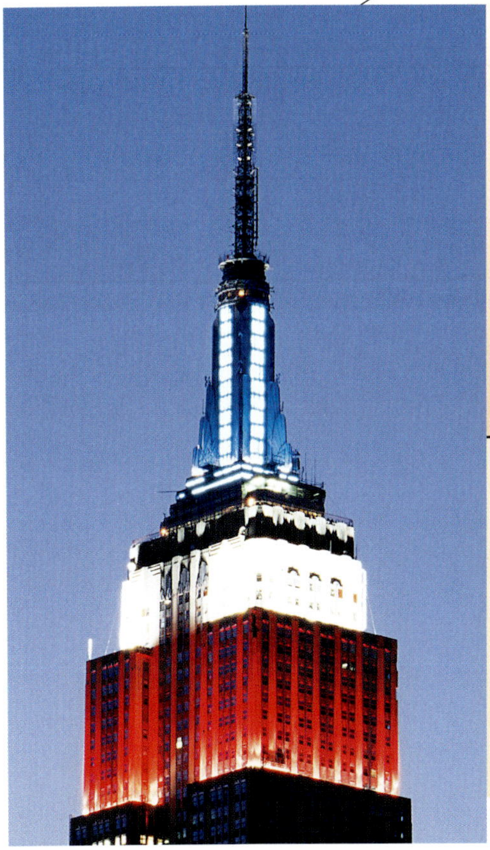

Photo © Patrick Batchelder

FACT: The first light to shine from atop the building was a beacon in November of 1932, which announced the election of Franklin D. Roosevelt as president of the United States. In 1956 four revolving beacon lights, called "Freedom Lights" were installed. The 1964 New York World's Fair brought new lighting to the building, with the top thirty floors being illuminated with a series of floodlights. Red, white and blue lights were introduced for America's Bicentennial in 1976. A year later a more advanced lighting system was employed that would allow for a wider range of colors to be used.

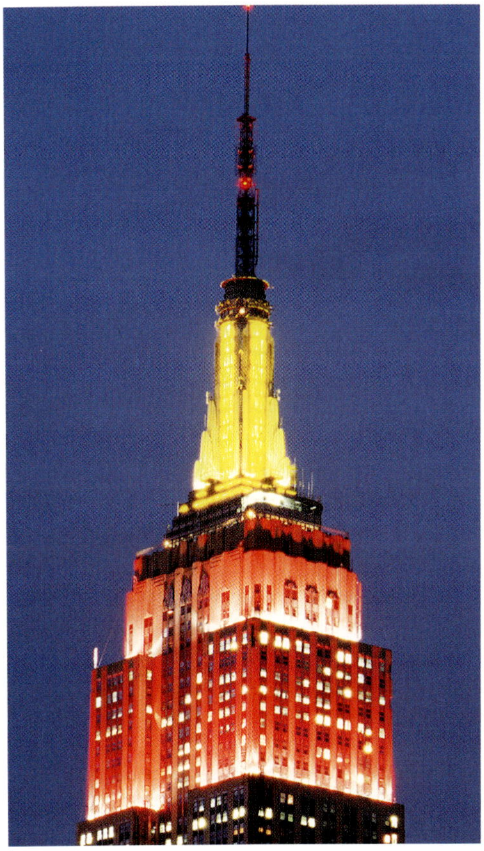

Photo © Patrick Batchelder

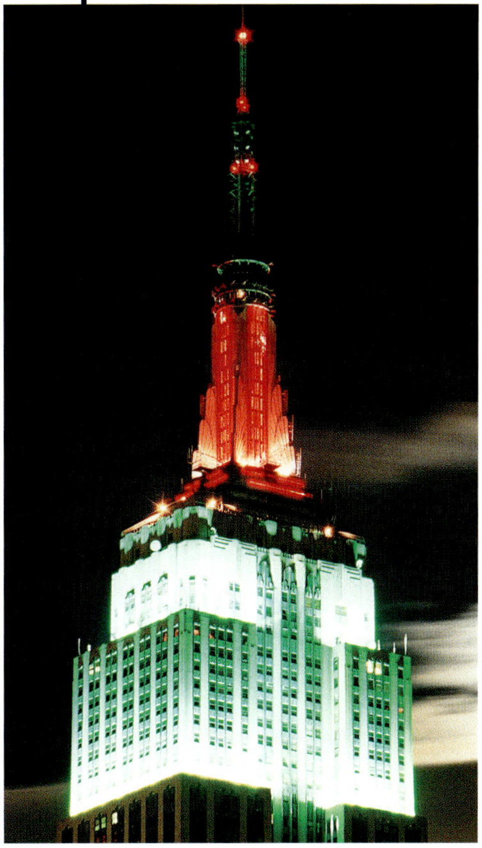

Photo © Grace Davies

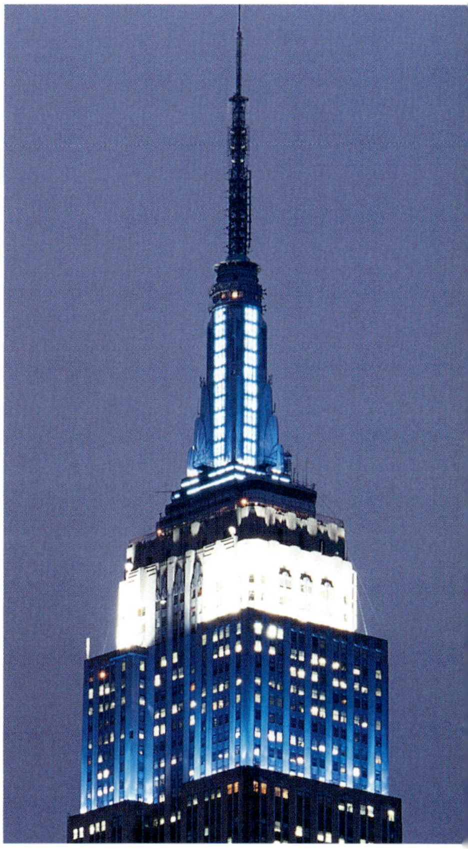

Photo © Patrick Batchelder

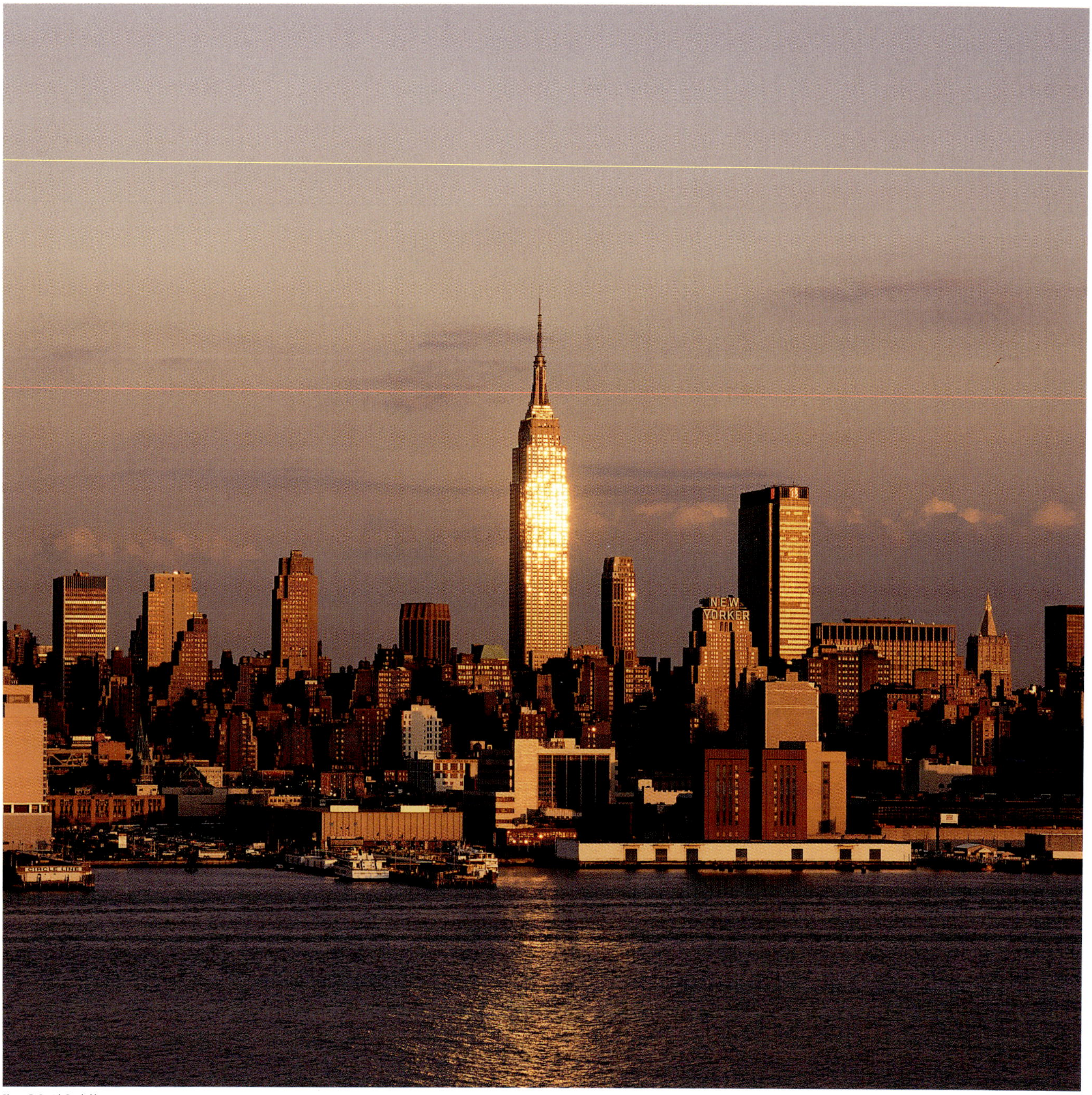

Photo © Patrick Batchelder

ABOVE: The view across the Hudson River can be a spectacular sight, especially when the setting sun is reflected on the windows of the Empire State Building. **RIGHT:** Looking northwest from the Lower East Side, a telephoto lens creates the illusion that the Empire State Building stands directly behind the Metropolitan Life Tower, even though it is ten blocks away.

FOLLOWING PAGES, LEFT: Chain-link fence and older buildings provide a different perspective to the Empire State Building. **TOP RIGHT:** With the Manhattan Bridge in the foreground, night falls on the city as seen from the Brooklyn Bridge. **BOTTOM RIGHT:** Travelling up the East River, a Circle Line Ferry is soon to be passing under the Brooklyn Bridge.

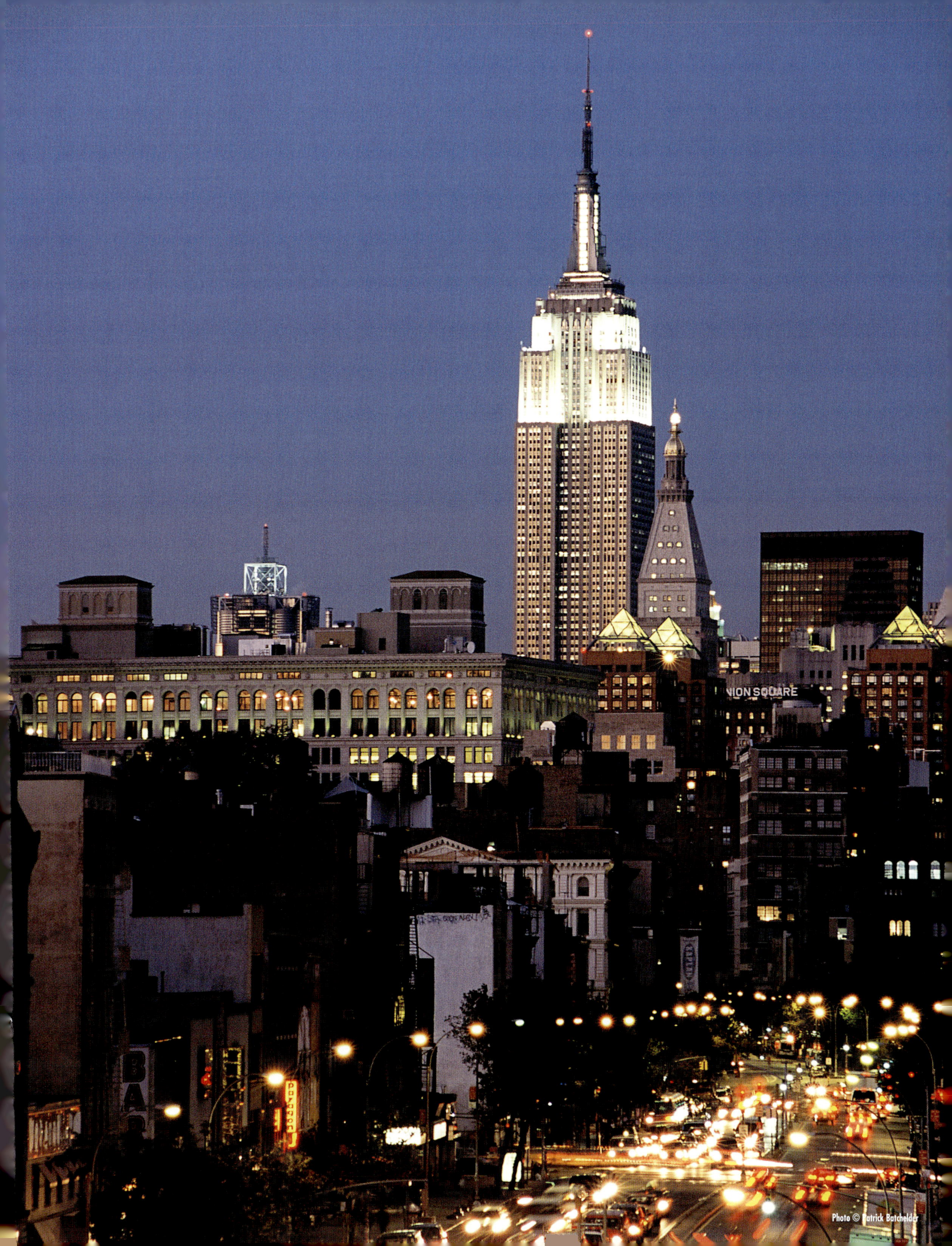

Photo © Patrick Batchelder

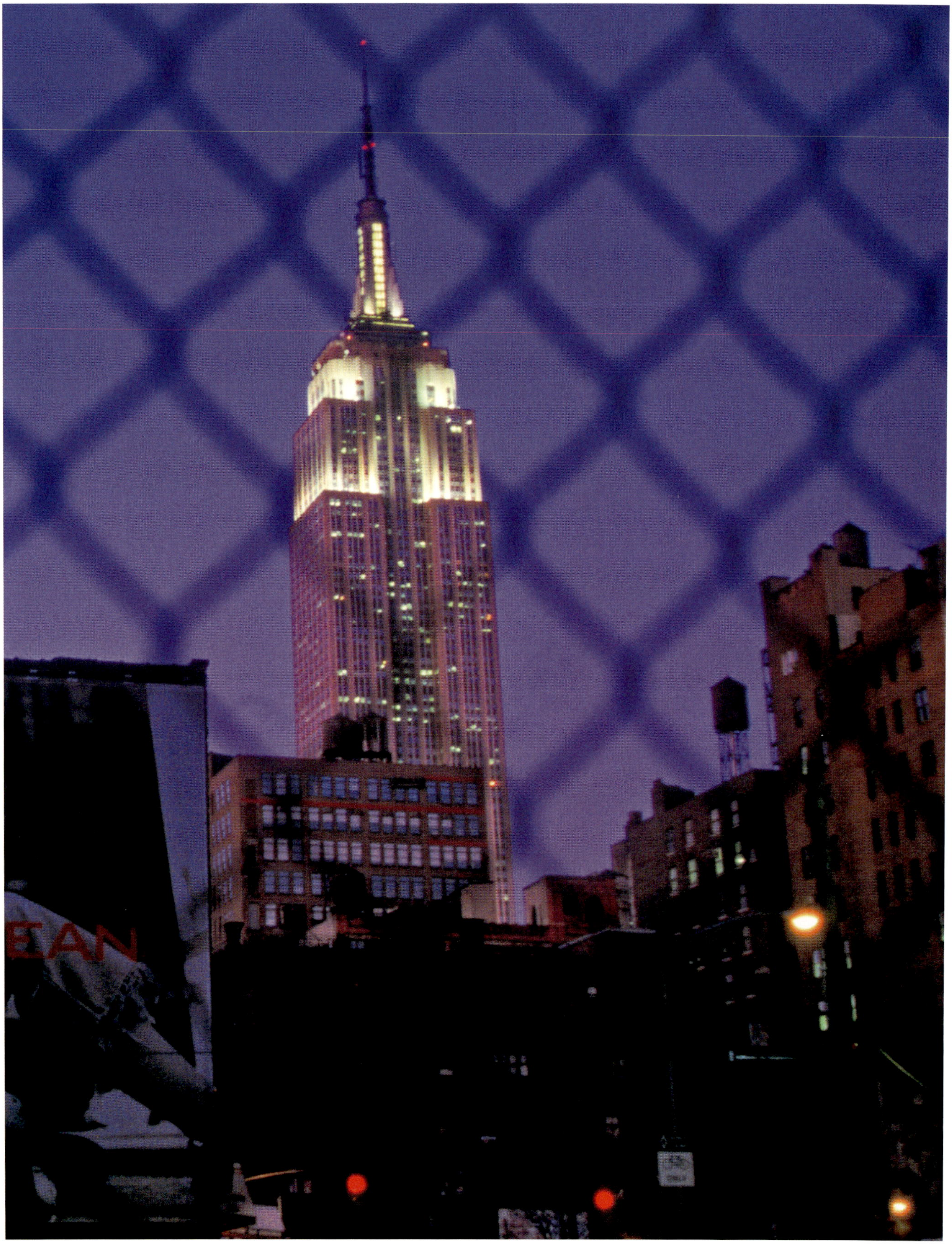

Photo © Jim West

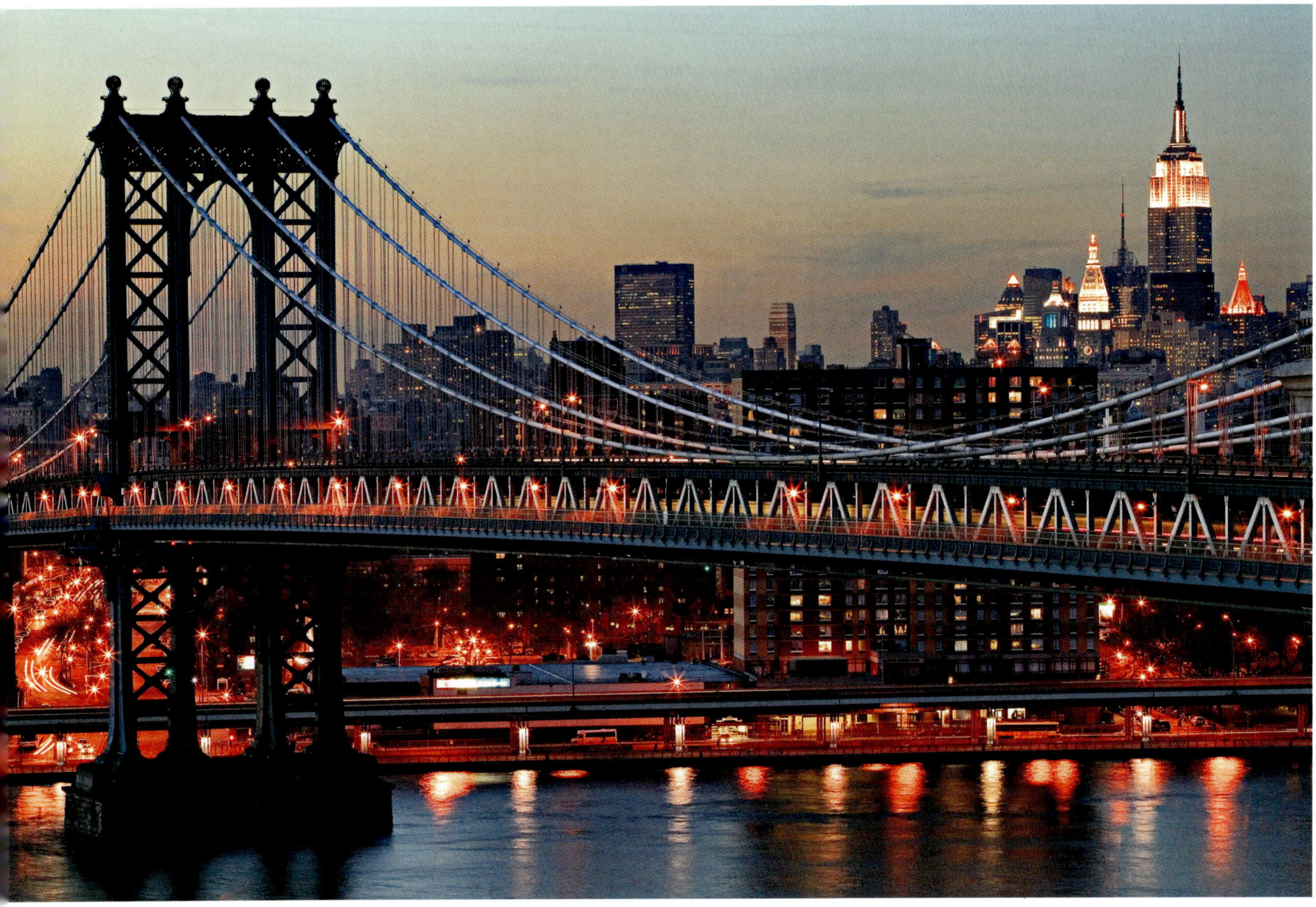

Photo © Jon Arnold/DanitaDelimont.com

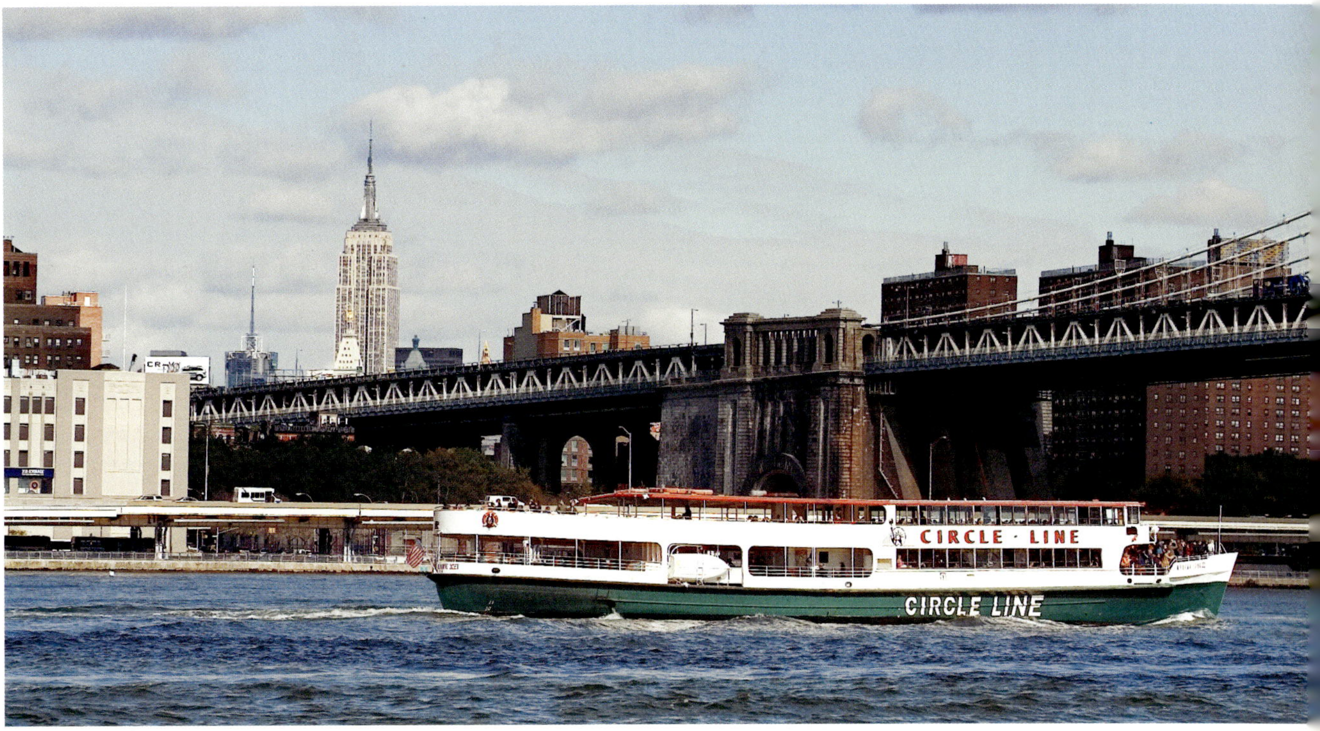

Photo by Joe Luman © Terrell Creative

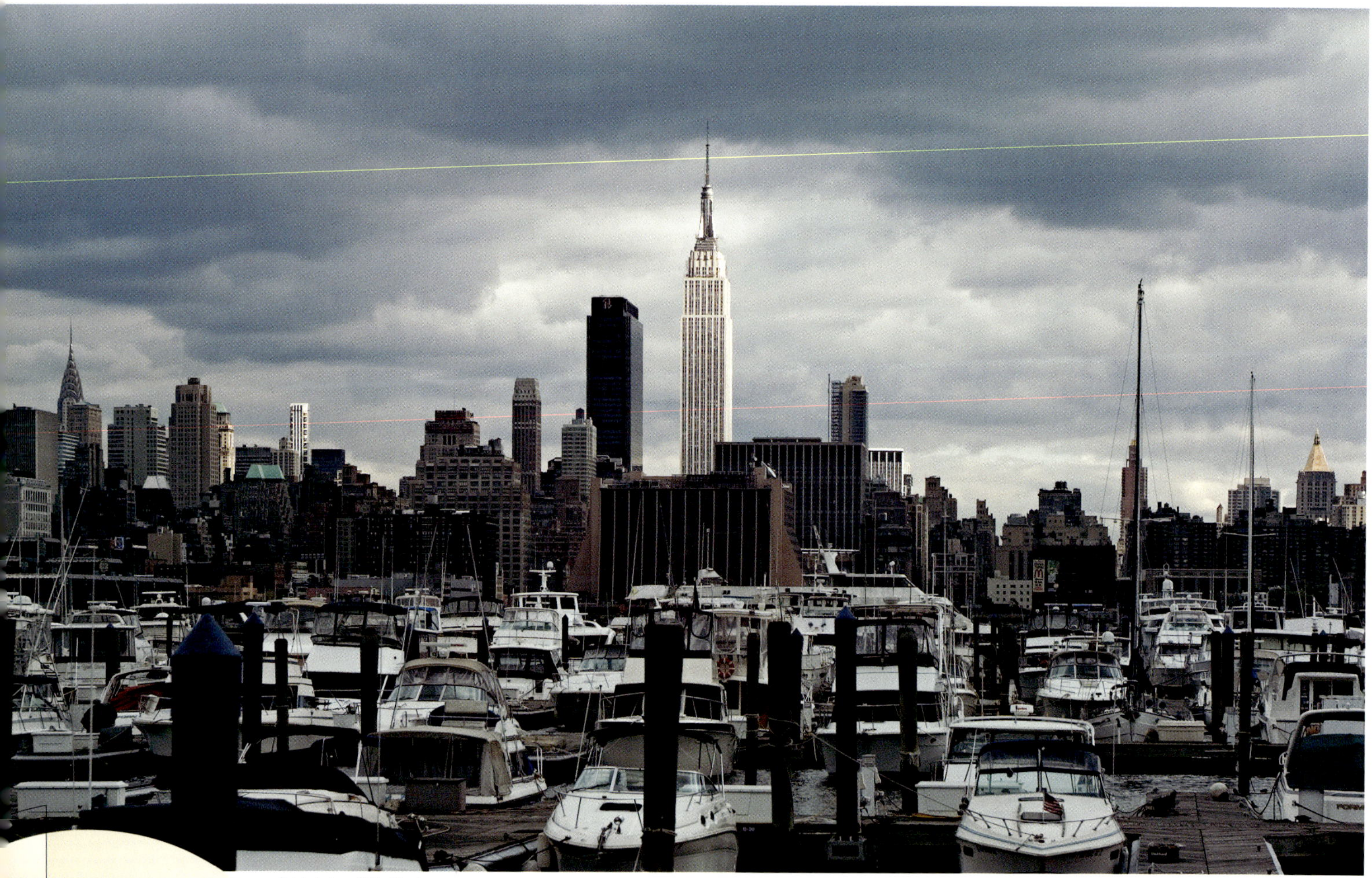

Photo by Joe Luman © Terrell Creative

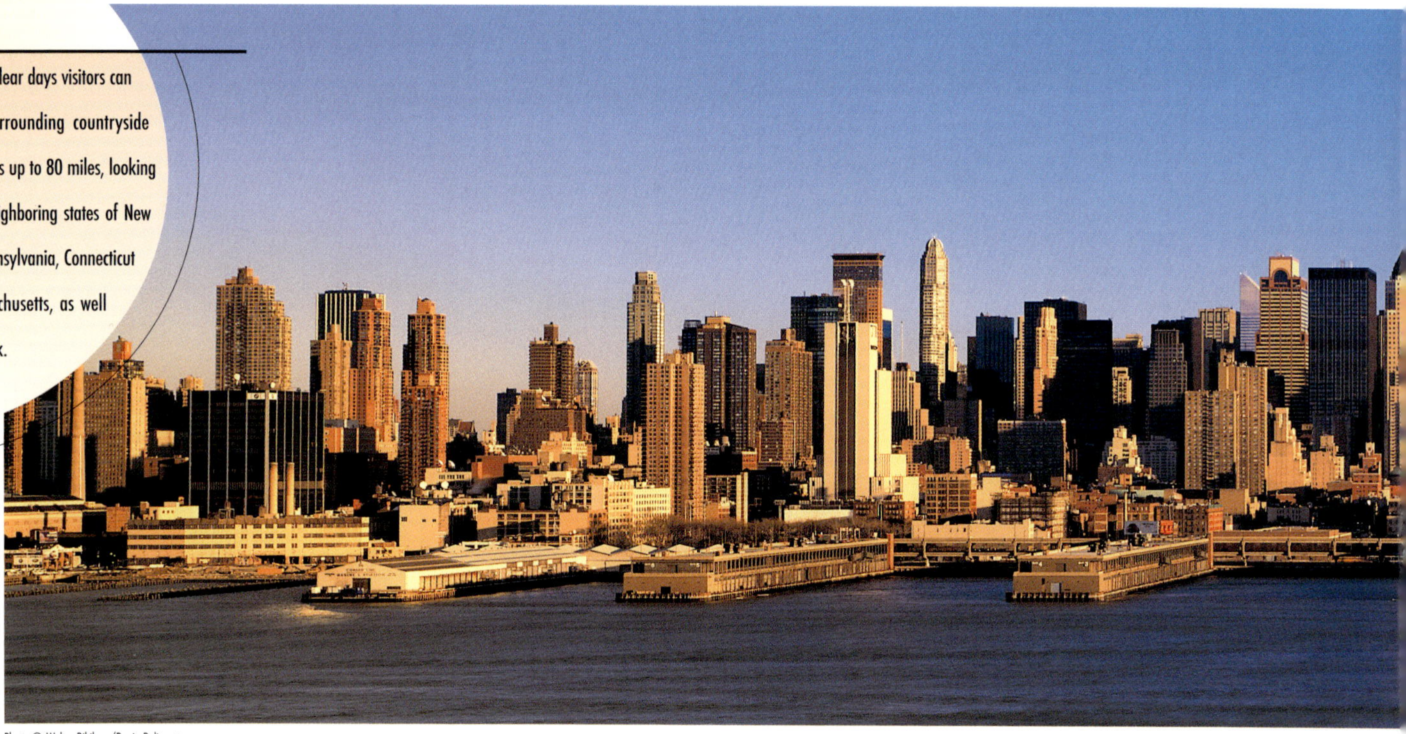

Photo © Walter Bibikow/DanitaDelimont.com

FACT: On clear days visitors can see the surrounding countryside for distances up to 80 miles, looking into the neighboring states of New Jersey, Pennsylvania, Connecticut and Massachusetts, as well as New York.

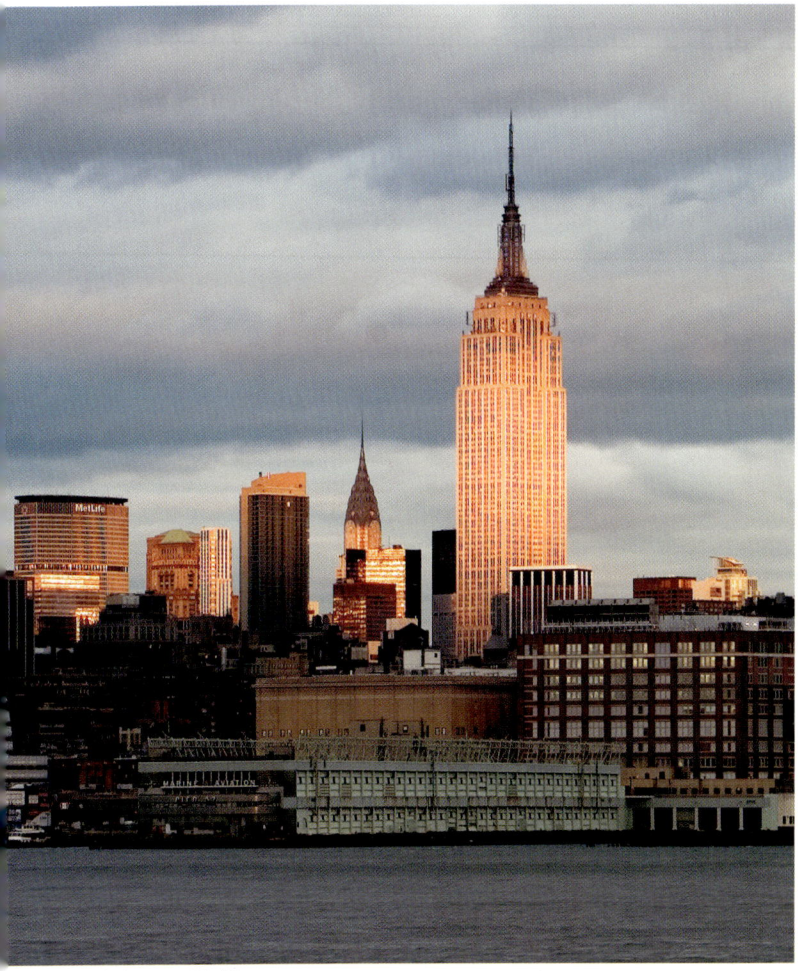

Photo by Joe Luman © Terrell Creative

FAR LEFT: The sun breaks through on an overcast day to shine its light only on the Empire State Building in this view taken from a marina on the Hudson River in Weehawken, New Jersey. **LEFT:** The sun illuminates everything but the very top of the tower of the Empire State Building in this photo taken from Hoboken, New Jersey. The Chrysler Building is basking in sun in the background. **BELOW:** This wide-angle aerial view was taken from above Union City, New Jersey, looking east across the Hudson River to Midtown Manhattan.

FOLLOWING PAGES, LEFT: The corner of 8th Avenue and 34th Street bustles at sunrise. **RIGHT:** Madison Square Garden stands to the west of the Empire State Building. This view is from the corner of 8th Avenue and 33rd Street.

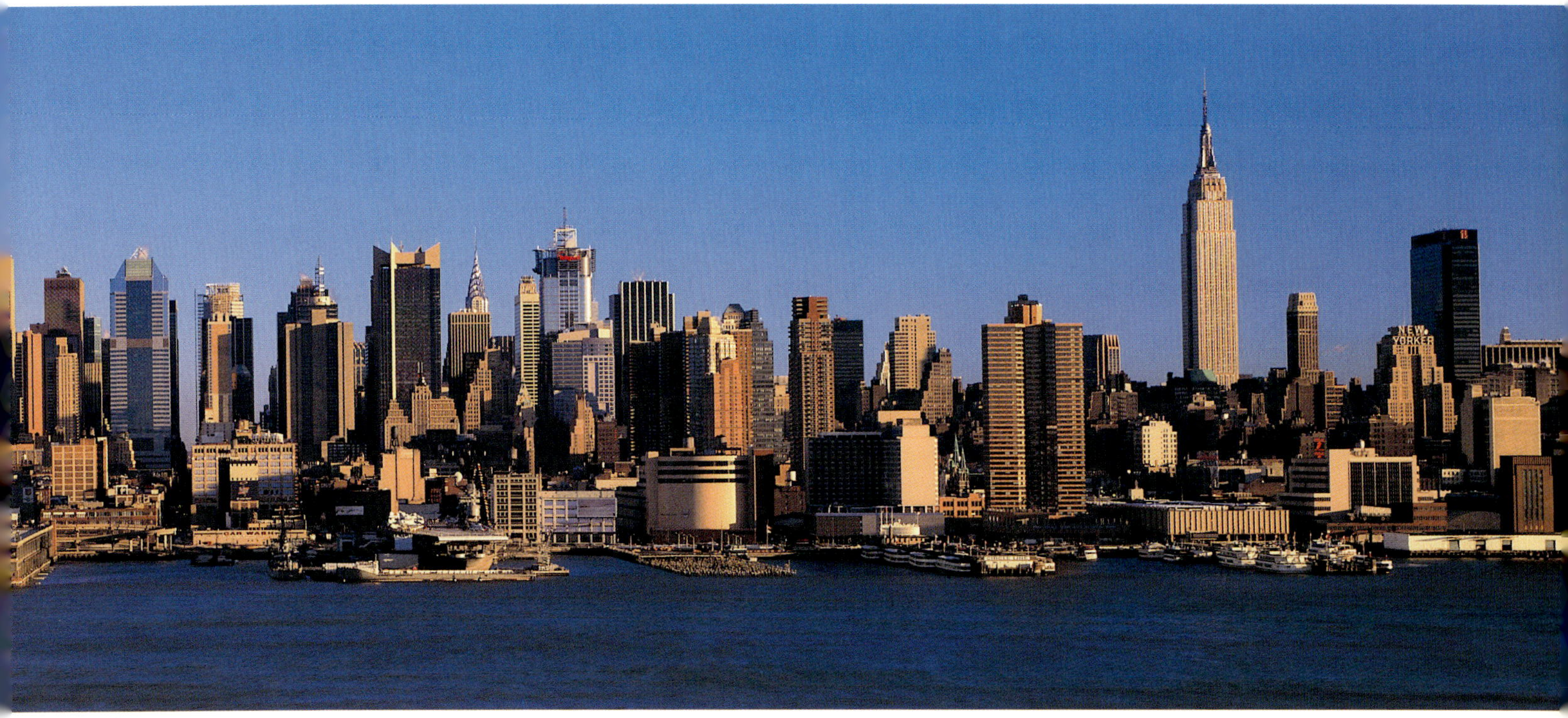

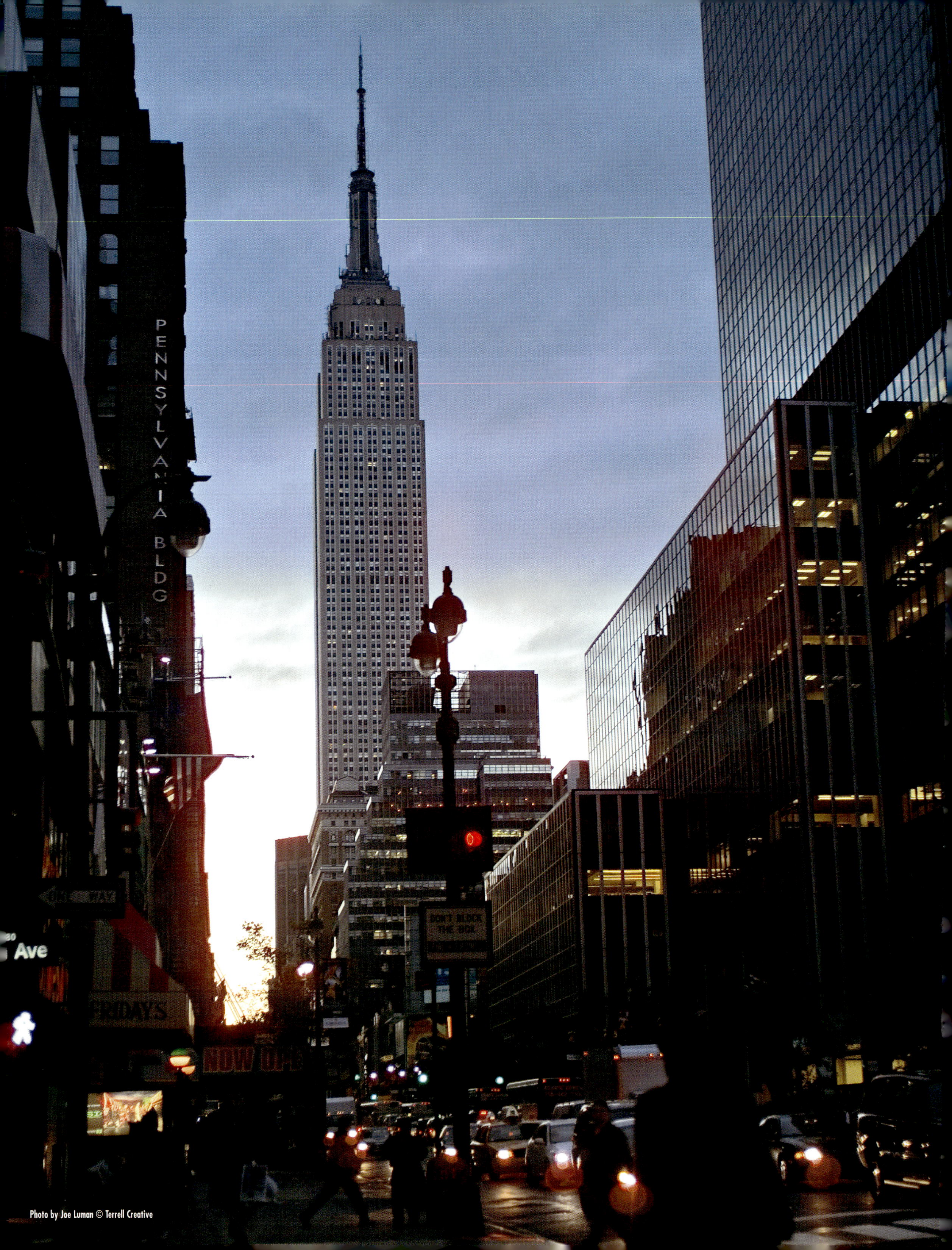

Photo by Joe Luman © Terrell Creative

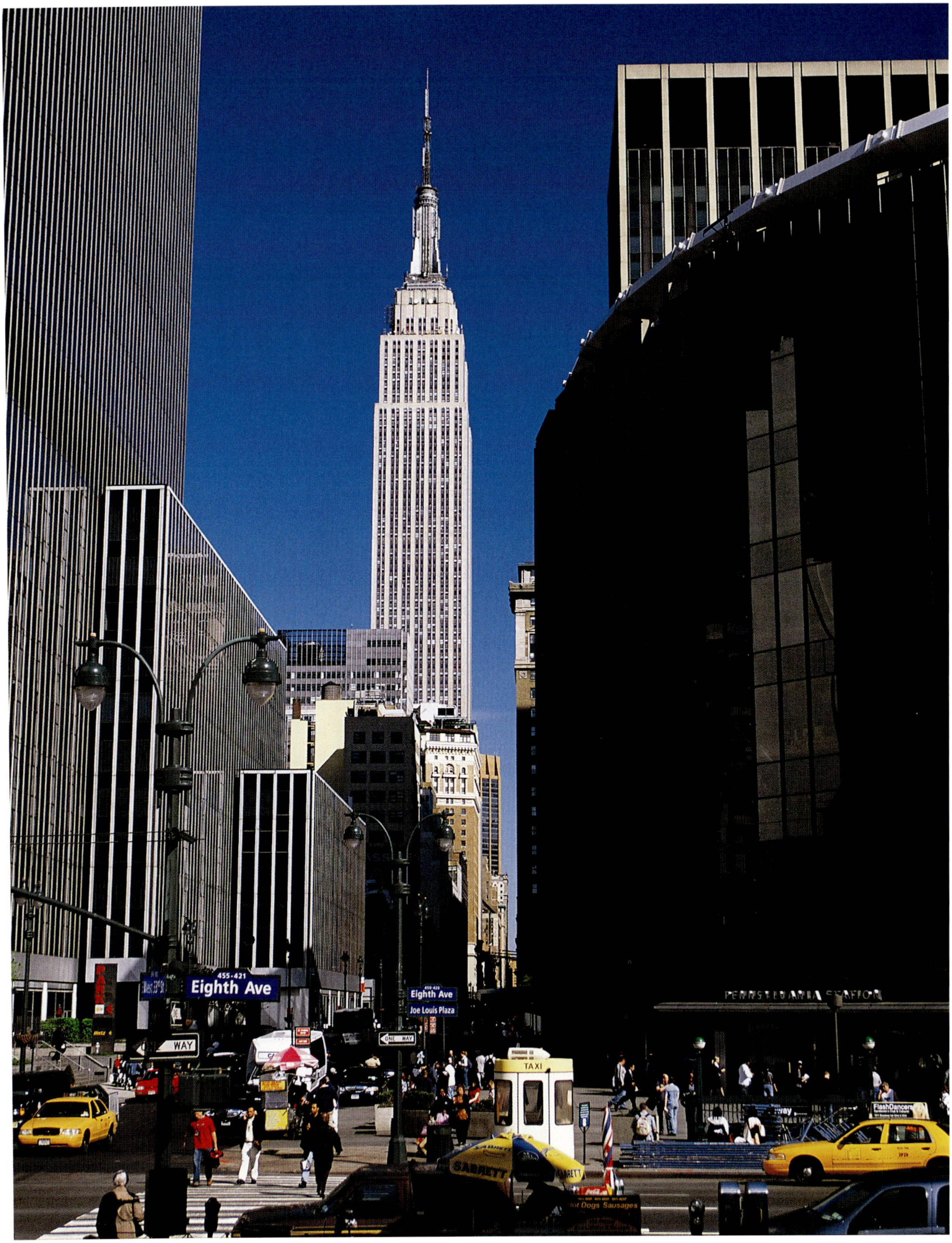

Photo © Patrick Batchelder

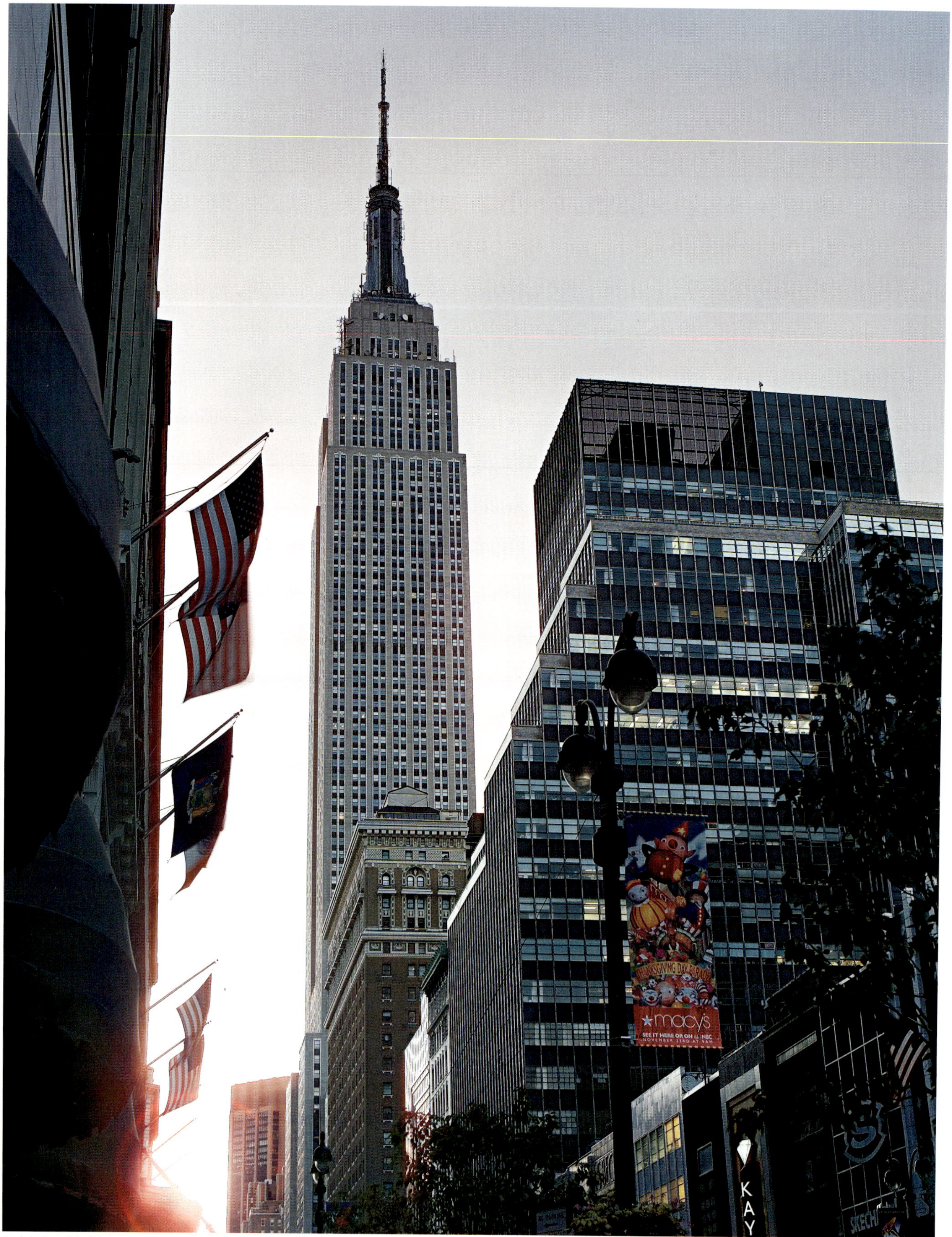

Photo by Joe Luman © Terrell Creative

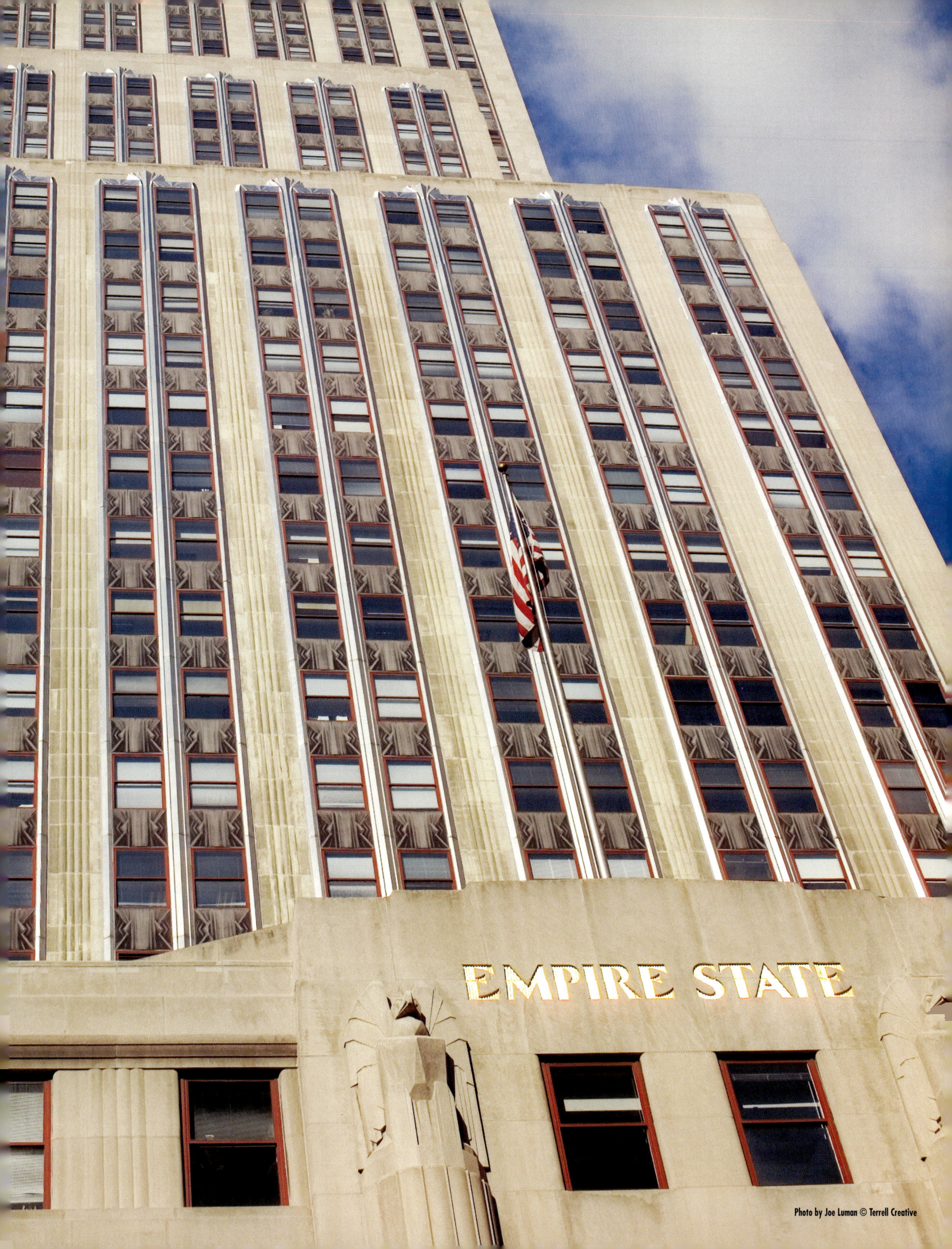

Photo by Joe Luman © Terrell Creative

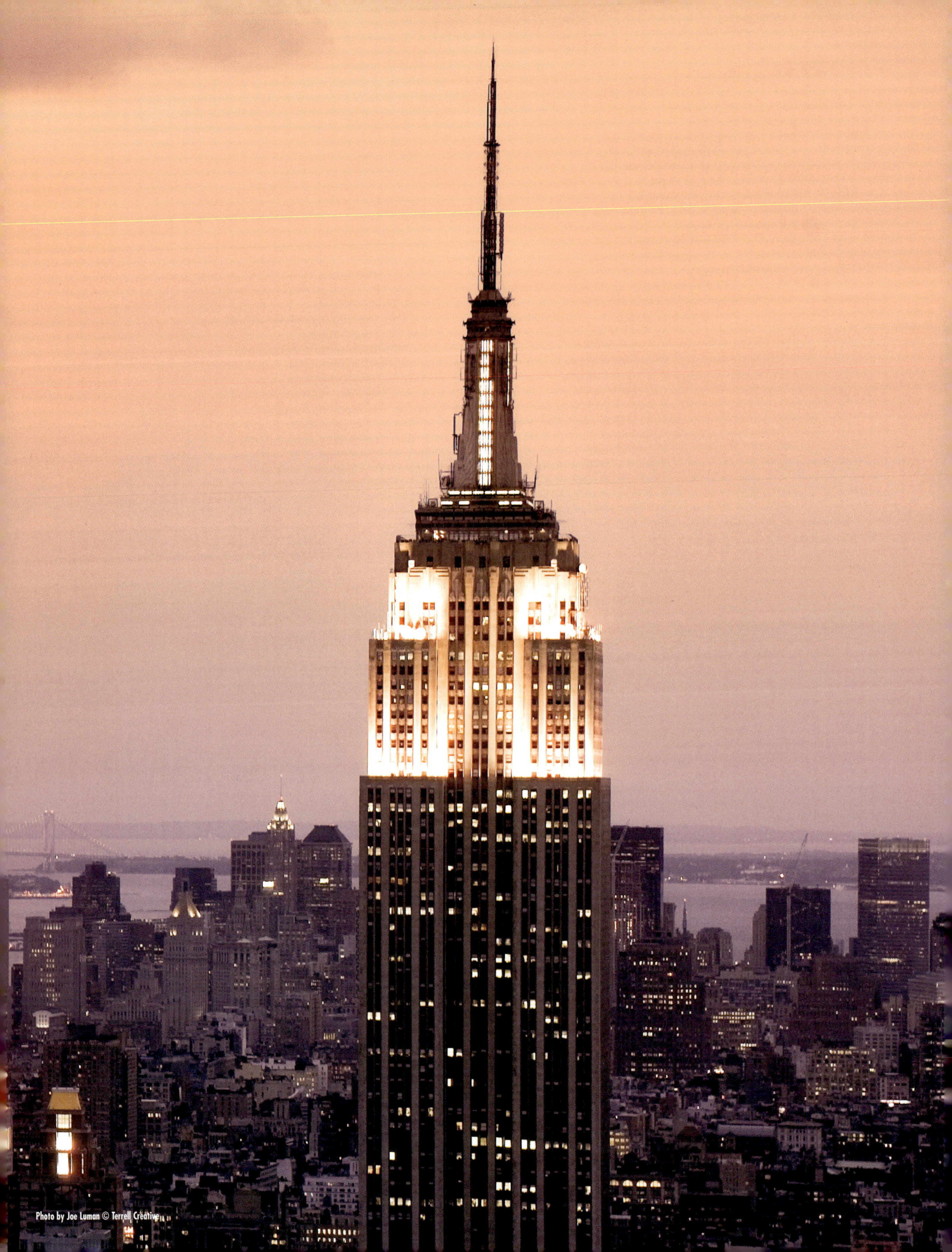

Photo by Joe Luman © Terrell Creative

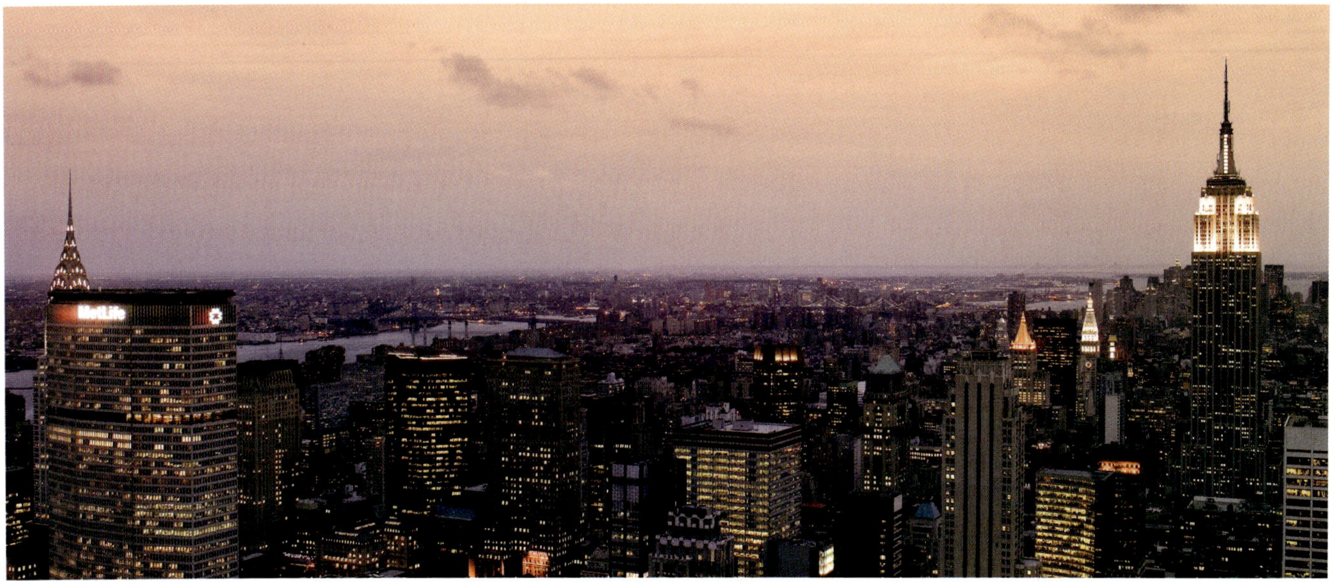

Photo by Joe Luman © Terrell Creative

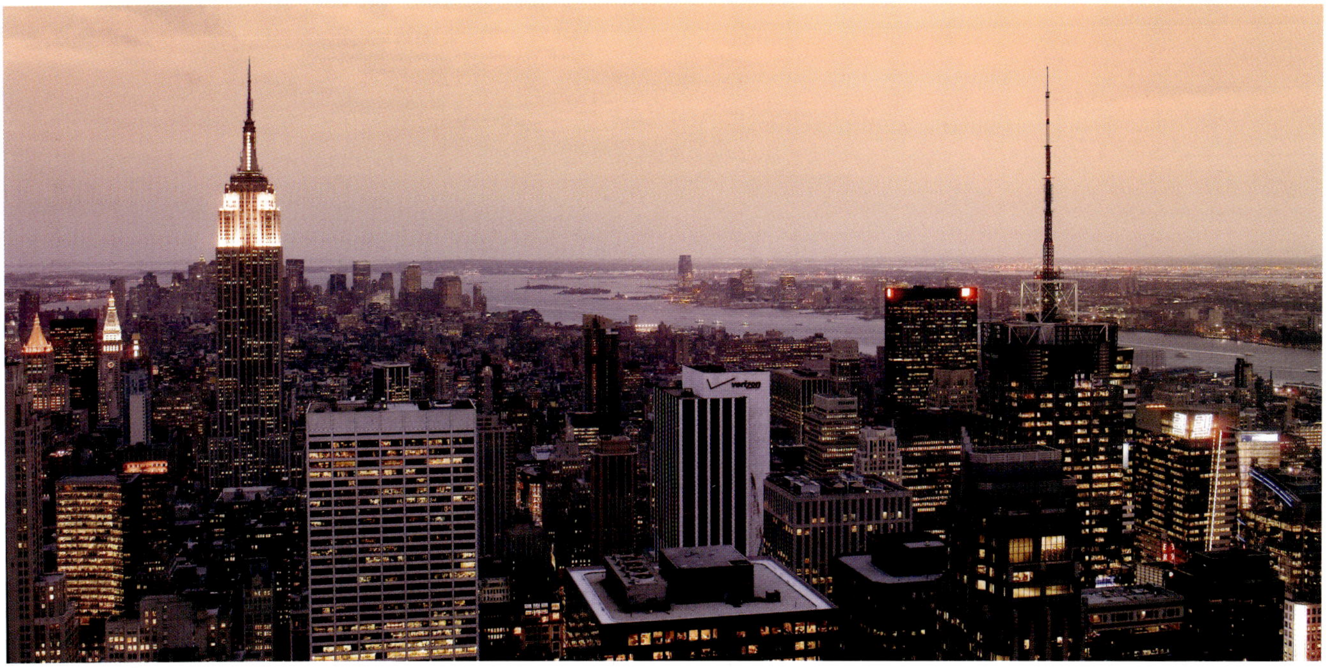

Photo by Joe Luman © Terrell Creative

PREVIOUS PAGES, LEFT: Looking east on 34th Street the sun breaks across the horizon silhouetting the Empire State Building in a white glow. **RIGHT:** The noonday sun bathes the 34th Street façade of the Empire State Building.

LEFT: The observation deck of the GE Building, 30 Rockefeller Plaza, affords breathtaking views of the Empire State Building. Here the telephoto lens provides a close-up view of the illuminated top 30 floors. The financial district is seen in the background with a portion of the Verrazano-Narrows Bridge visible in the distance. **ABOVE TOP:** Looking southeast from the GE Building, the Chrysler Building is on the far left and the Empire State Building is at the far right of this photo. **ABOVE BOTTOM:** Looking southwest from the GE Building, Times Square is on the right and the Empire State Building in on the left.

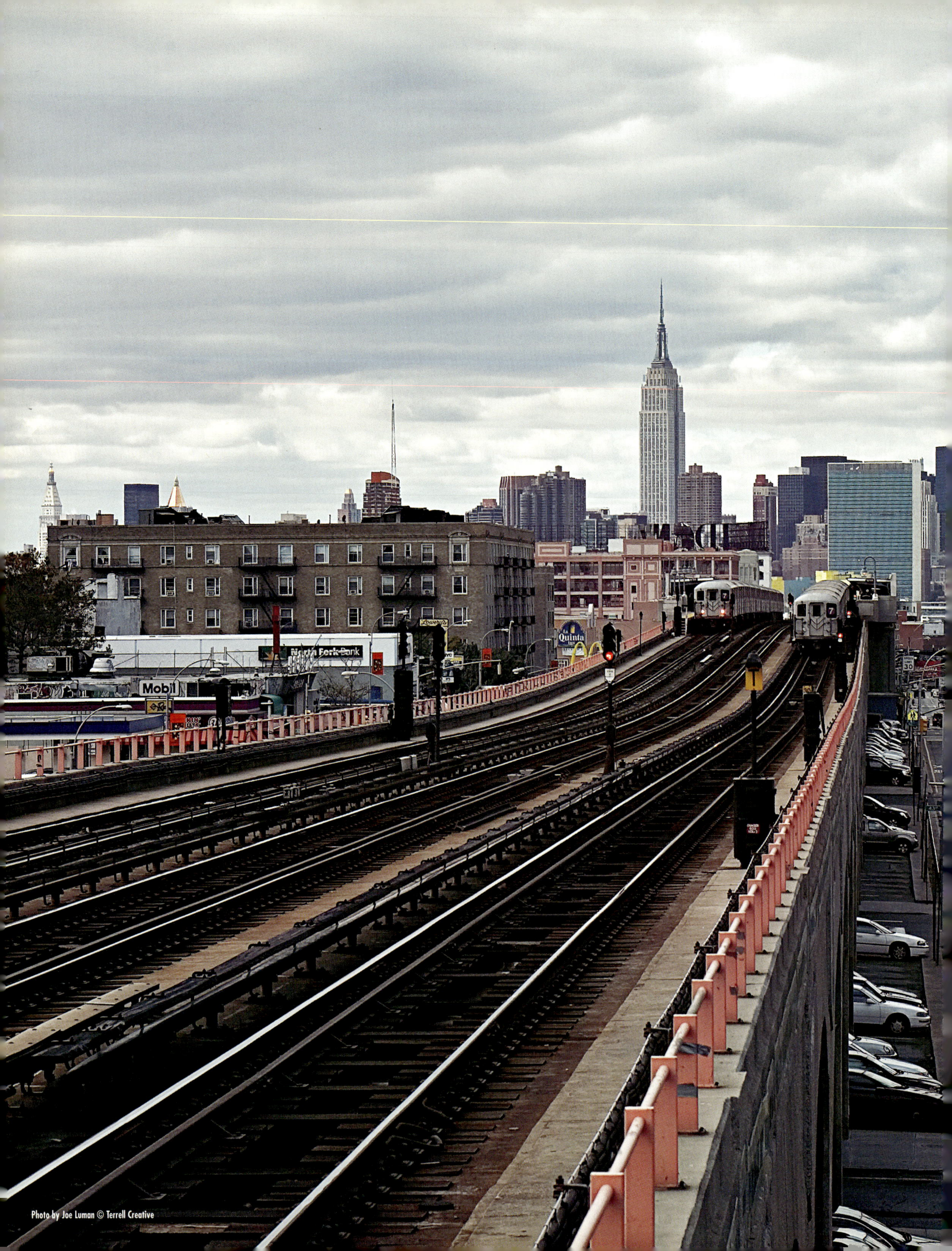

Photo by Joe Luman © Terrell Creative

FACT: Pennies tossed from the 86th floor observation deck will never reach the street below. The numerous recesses on the tower's façade will naturally collect objects dropped from above. Wind currents push objects against the face of the building, which also accounts for the apparent "upward travel" of rain when storms are observed from the upper floors.

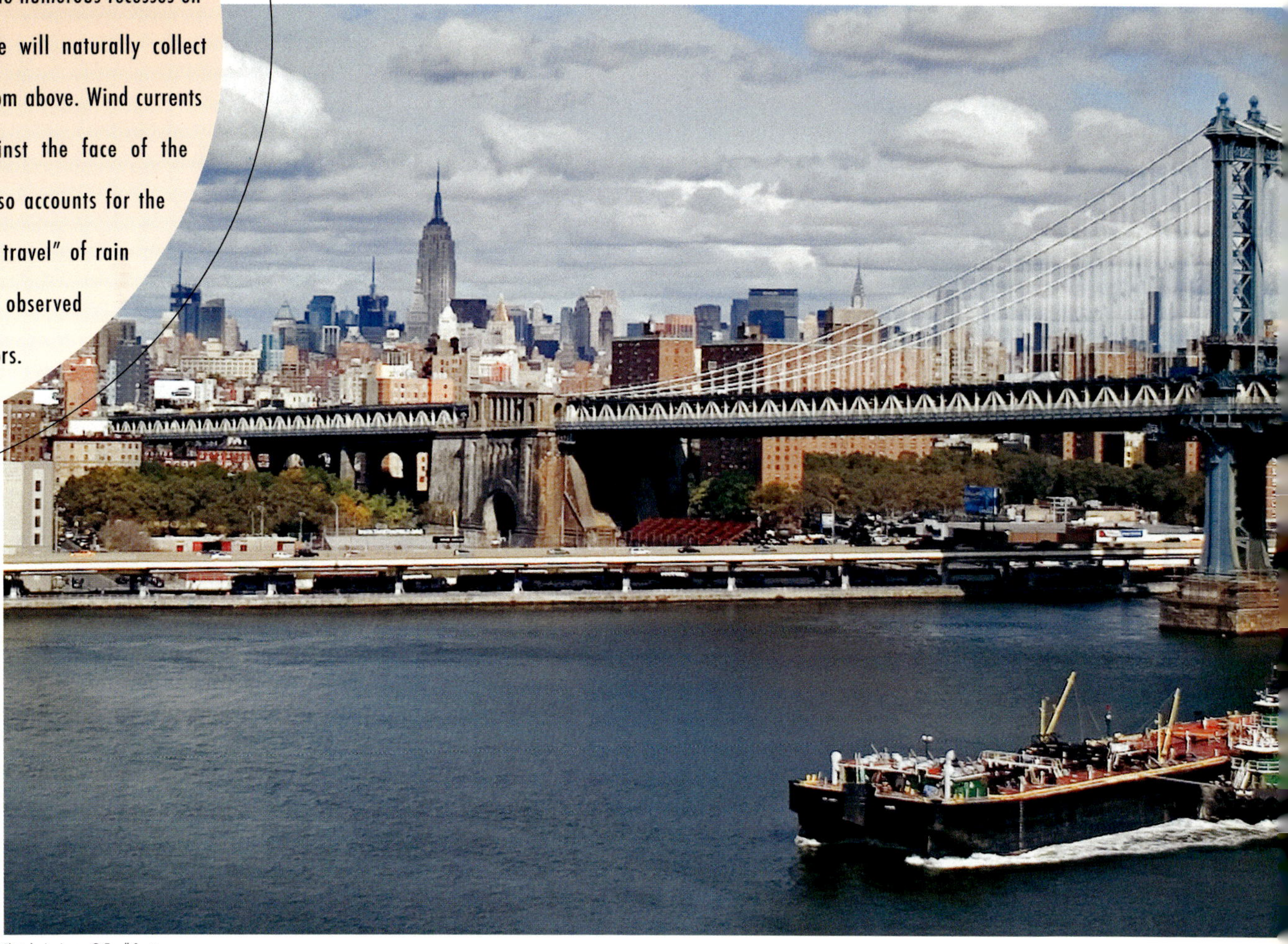

Photo by Joe Luman © Terrell Creative

LEFT: The 46th Street Station provides an interesting view west to the Empire State Building. This station is on the Queens Boulevard local line. **ABOVE:** A barge travels south on the East River in this photo taken from the Brooklyn Bridge. This vantage point allows a good view of the Manhattan Bridge and the midtown skyline beyond.

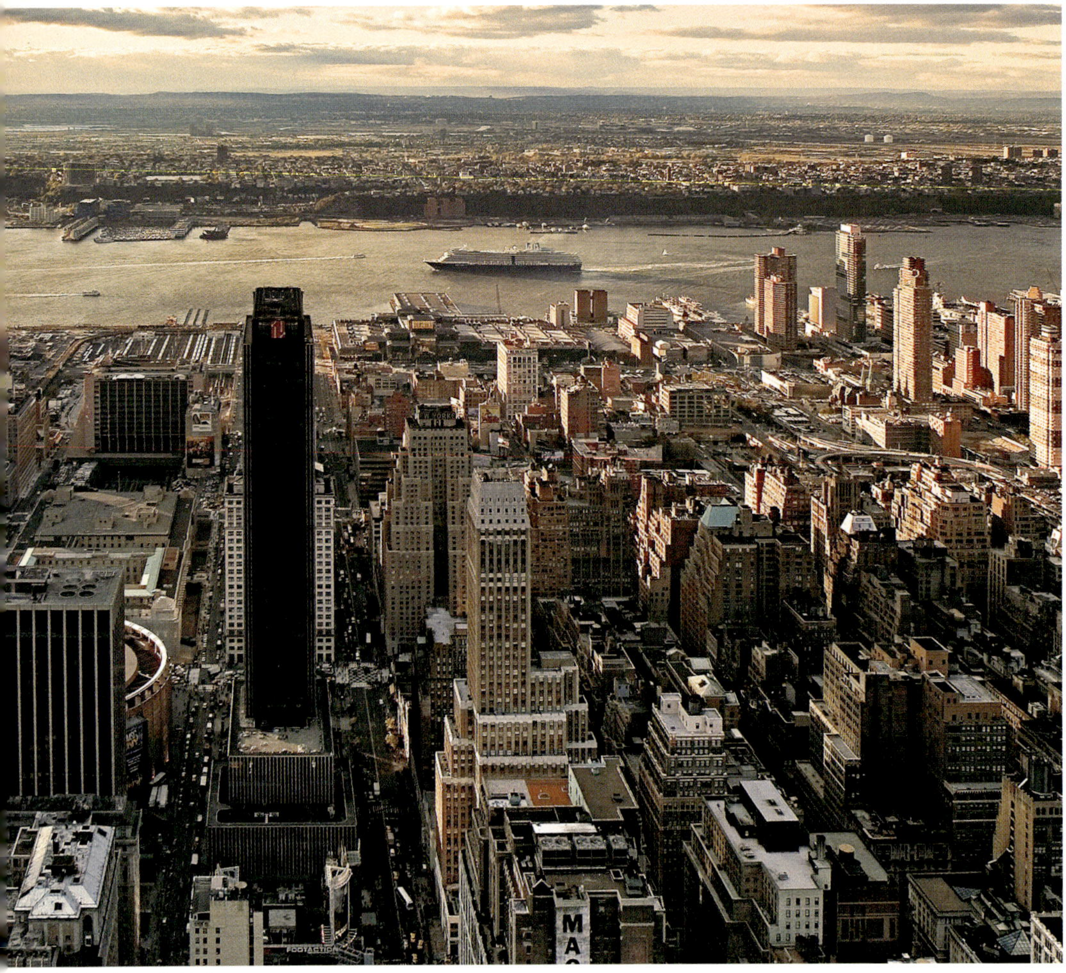

Photo by Joe Luman © Terrell Creative

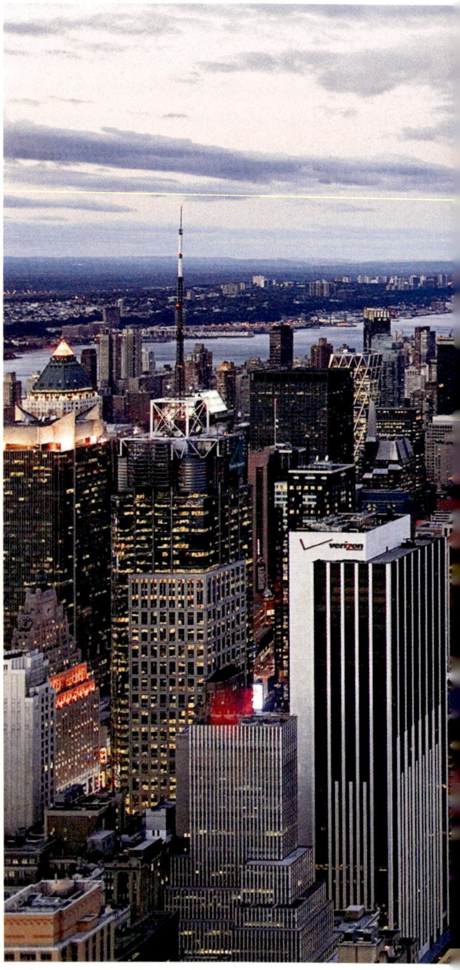

Photo by Joe Luman © Terrell Creative

ABOVE: Looking west from the 86th Floor Observatory a cruise ship is leaving port and heading down the Hudson River. Madison Square Garden is in view at the lower left. **ABOVE RIGHT:** At dusk the city quickly changes personalities. Looking north from the Empire State Building, Central Park is visible just beyond the GE Building. **BOTTOM RIGHT:** Looking northeast from the Empire State Building the central feature is the Chrysler Building. To the right along the East River is the United Nations Building. **BOTTOM FAR RIGHT:** The wedge-shaped Flatiron building is seen, looking south from the Empire State Building. This building is considered to be the first and oldest skyscraper in New York. Standing at 285 feet, it has been dwarfed by many buildings, especially the 1,472-foot Empire State Building

FOLLOWING PAGES, LEFT: The shadow of the Empire State Building is cast onto buildings on the northwest side of the tower. **RIGHT:** The early morning sun creates a red glow that reflects off of the 34th Street side of the Empire State Building.

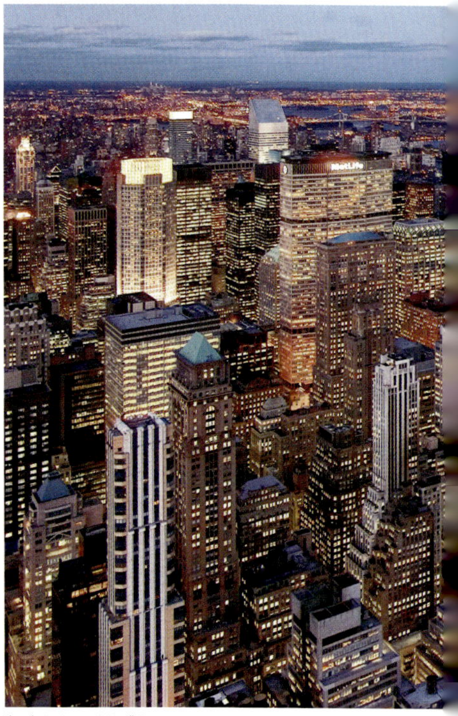

Photo by Joe Luman © Terrell Creative

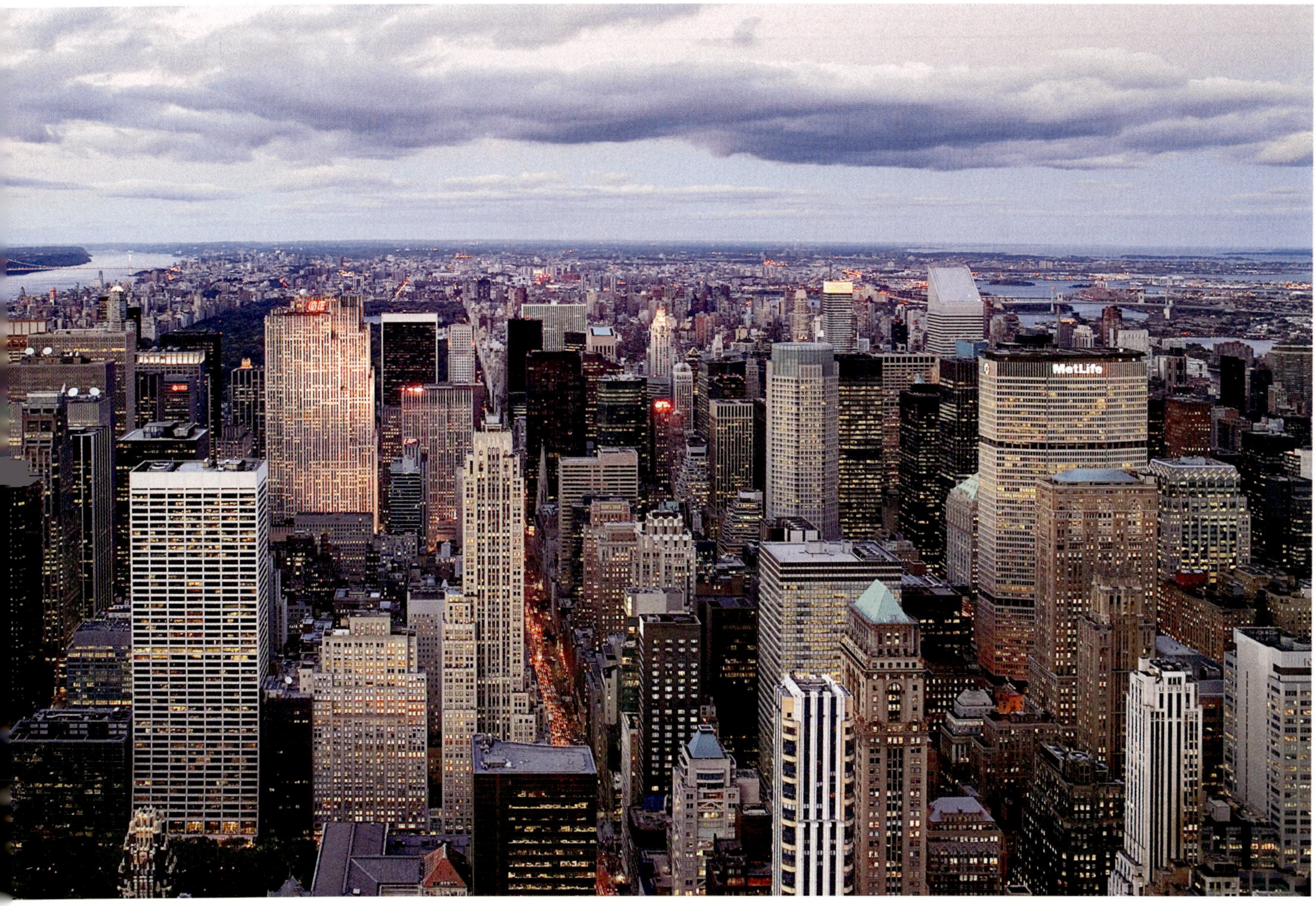

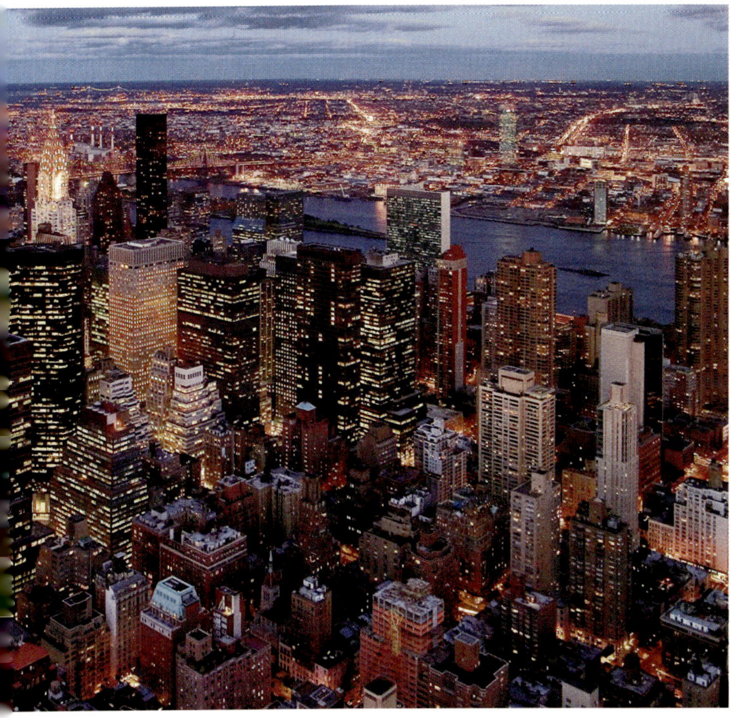

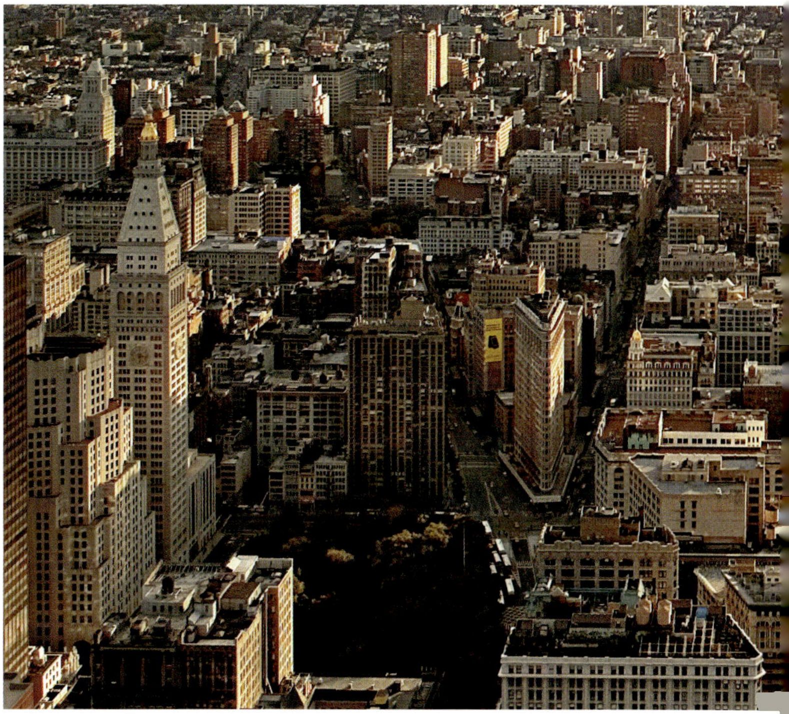

Photo by Joe Luman © Terrell Creative

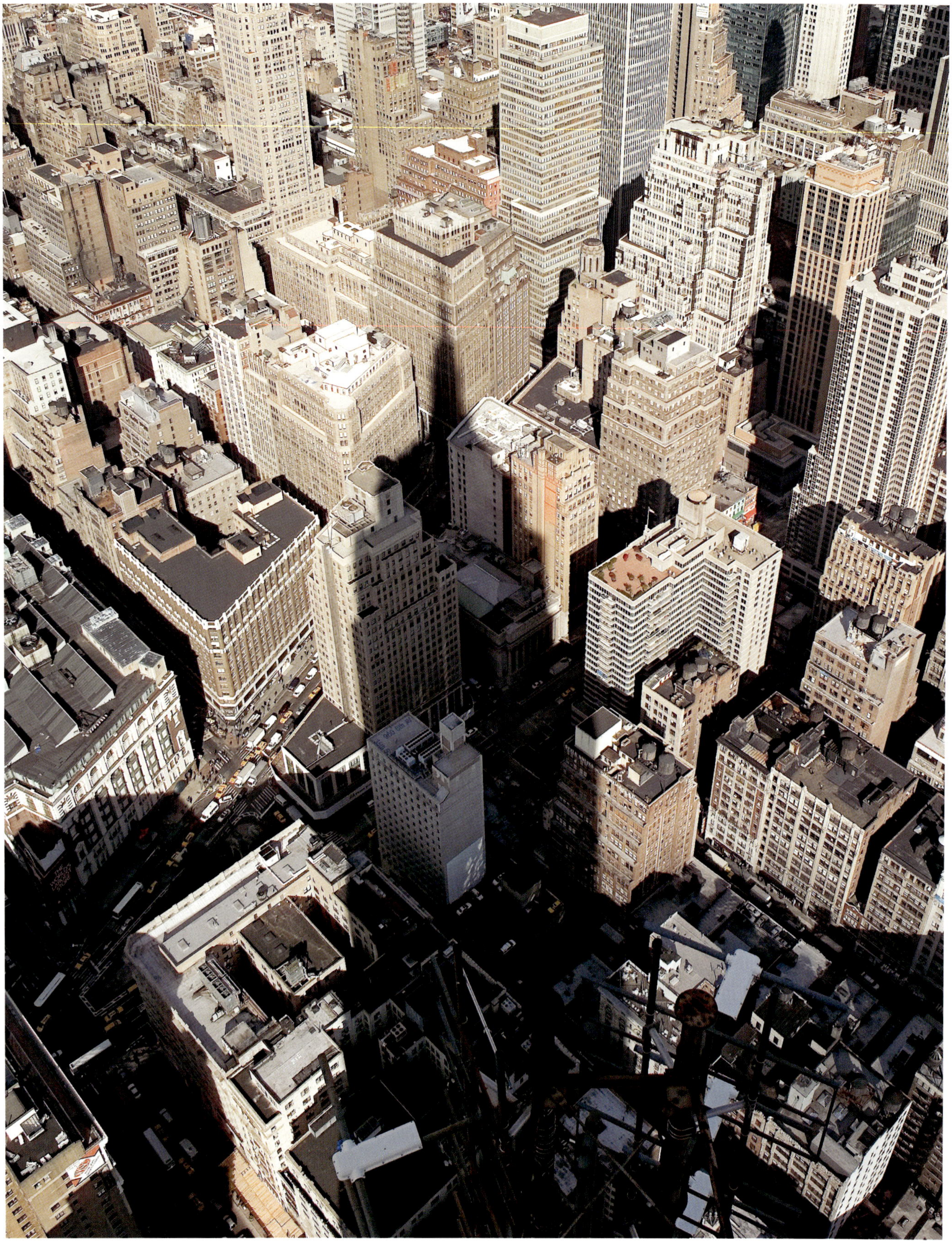

Photo by Joe Luman © Terrell Creative

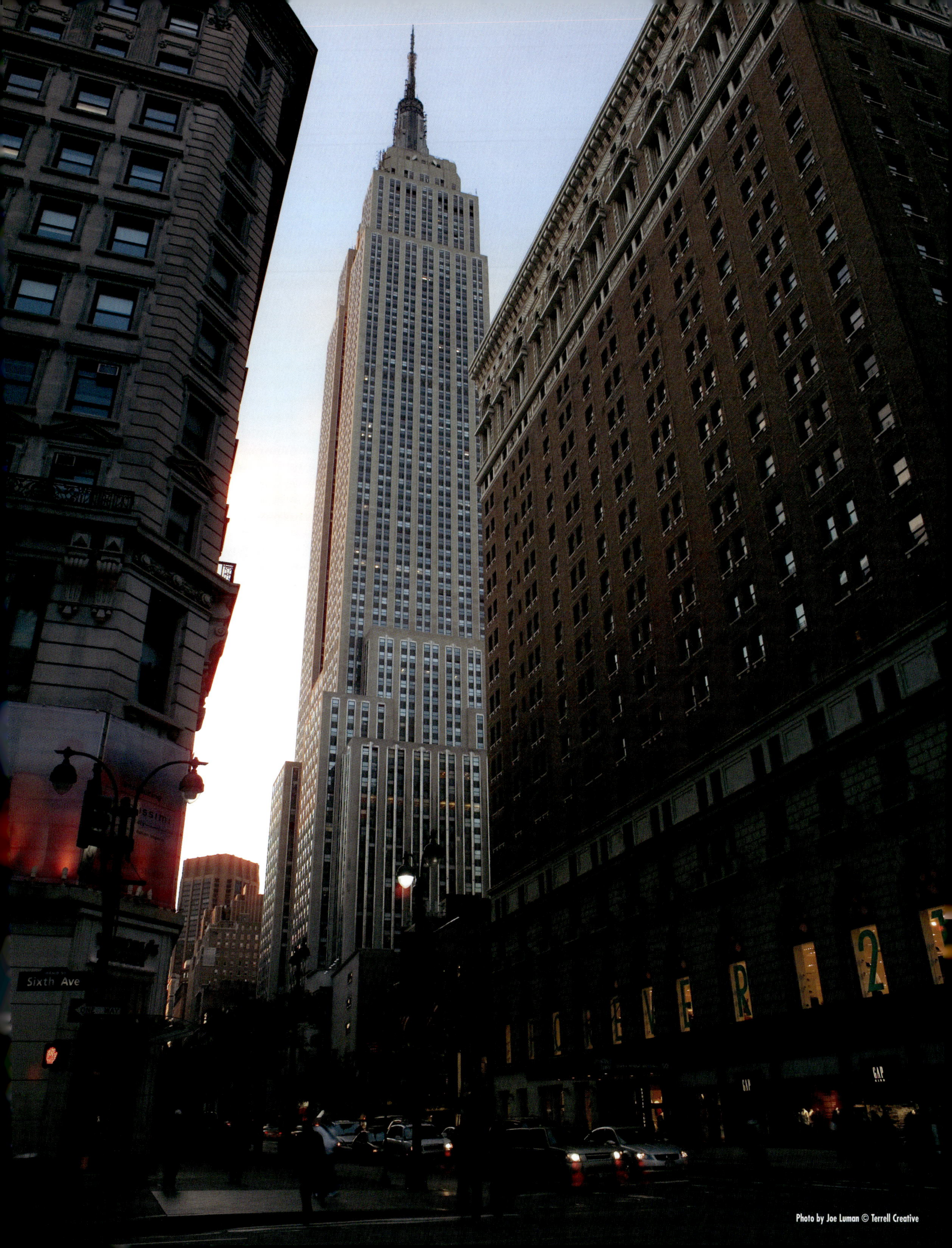

Photo by Joe Luman © Terrell Creative

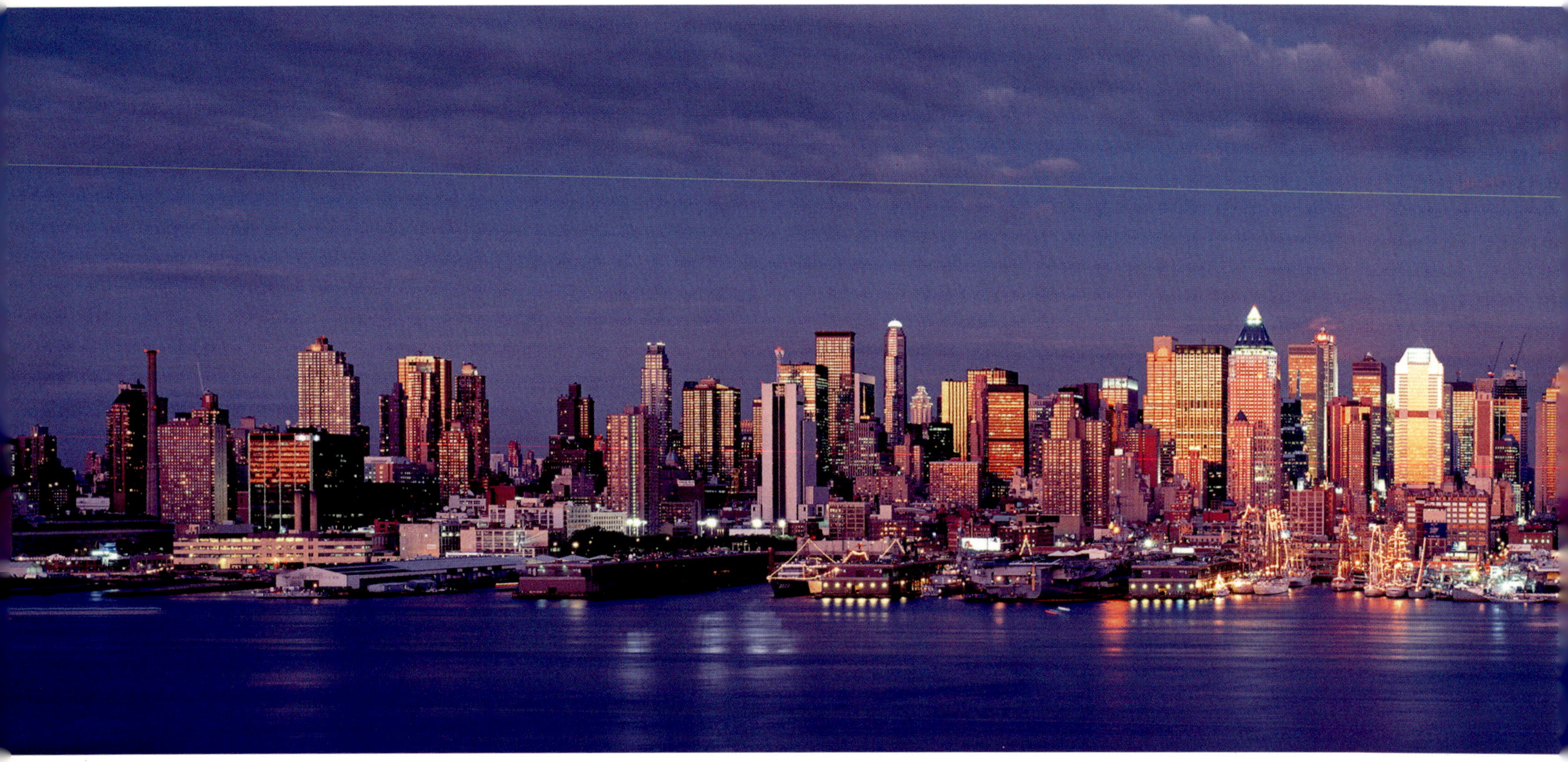

Photo © Richard Berenholtz

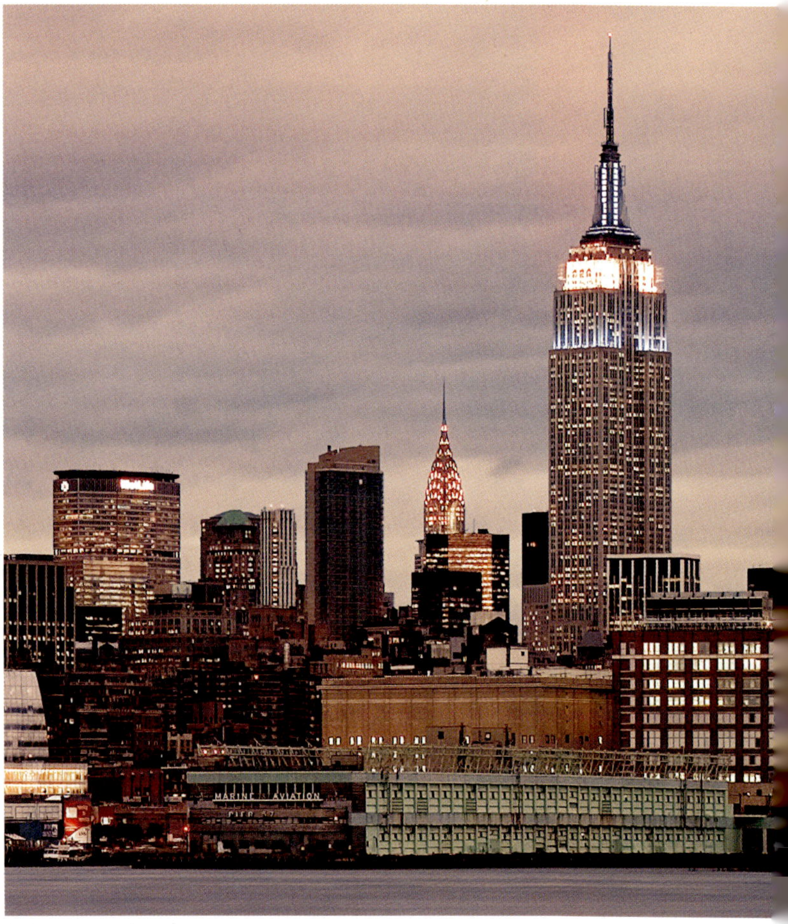

Photo by Joe Luman © Terrell Creative

ABOVE: This wide-angle photograph was taken from New Jersey from the vantage point of one of the high-rise condominiums that now line the western banks of the Hudson River. **RIGHT:** From this vantage point in Hoboken, the telephoto lens pulls the skyline closer in this photo taken at dusk.

FOLLOWING PAGES: The Empire State Building dominates the midtown skyline in this photo looking north, taken from the financial district.

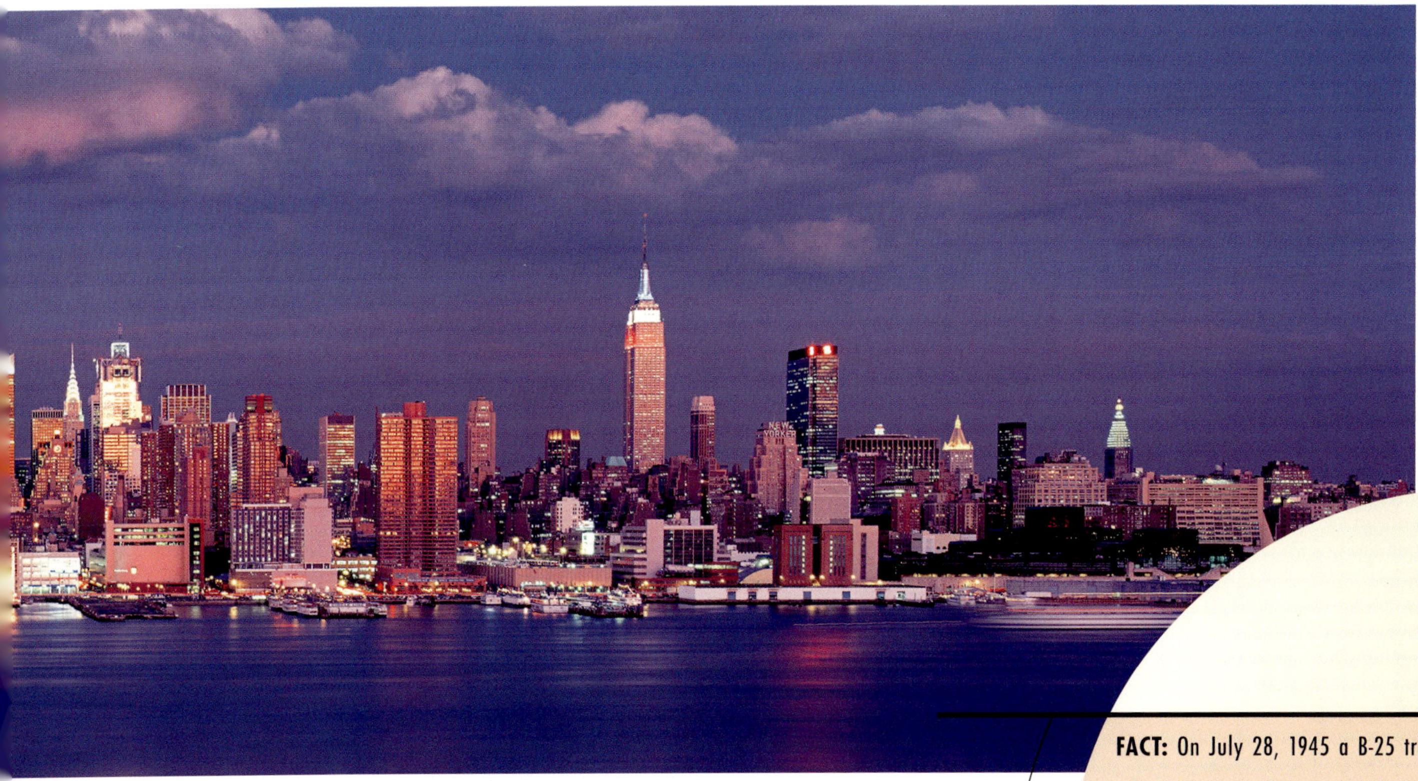

FACT: On July 28, 1945 a B-25 trainer bomber, lost in fog, flew into the Empire State Building, hitting the 79th floor. Loss of life was limited because the accident happened over a weekend, reducing the number of people that would otherwise have been in harm's way. Betty Lou Oliver, an elevator operator in the building, survived a 75-story free fall in an elevator after its damaged cables had snapped.

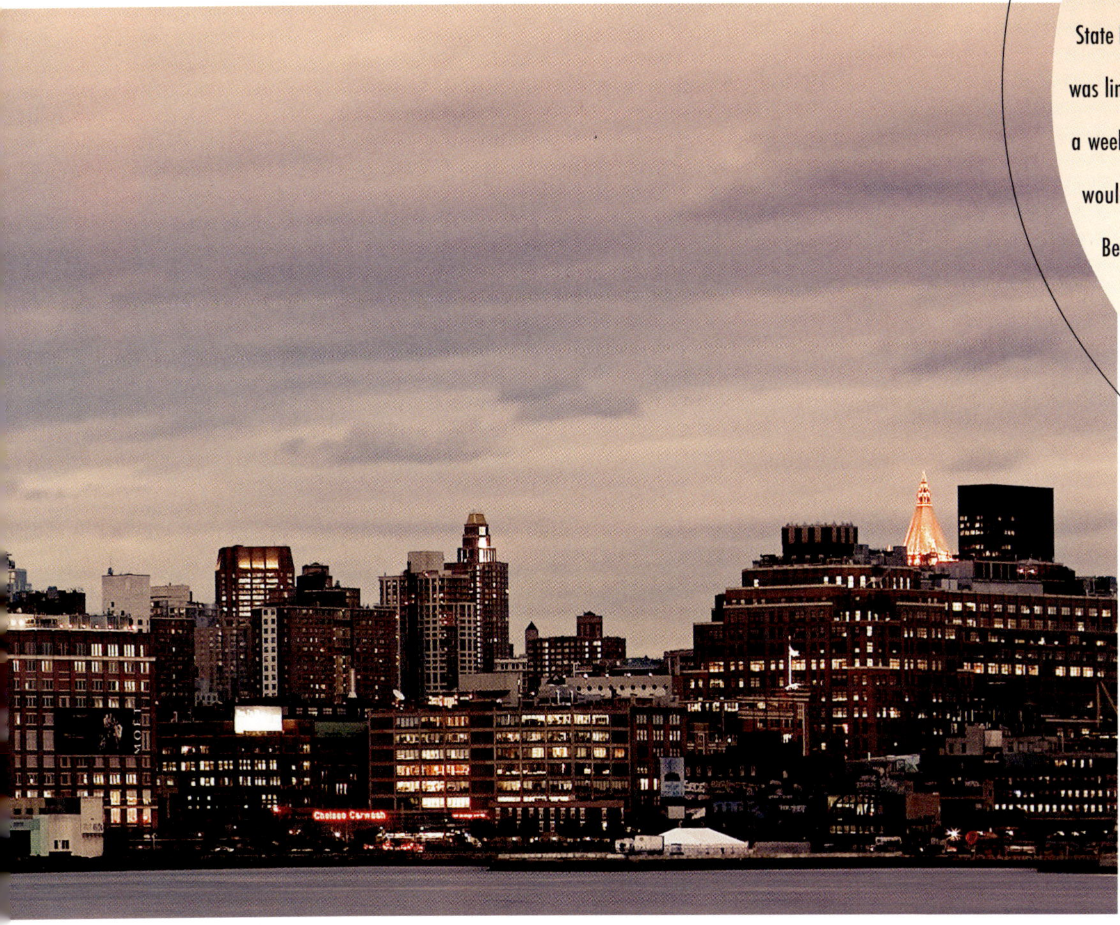

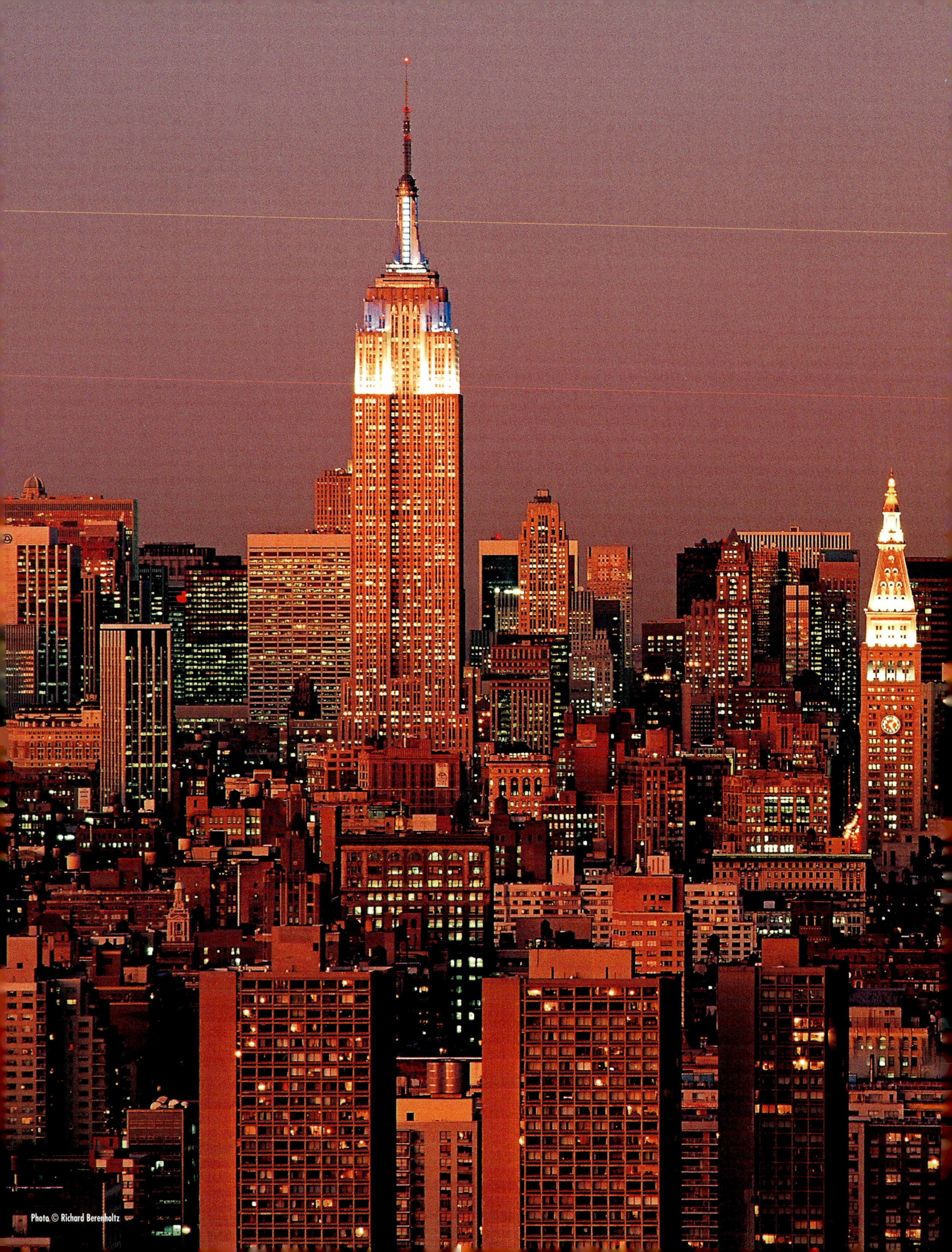
Photo © Richard Berenholtz

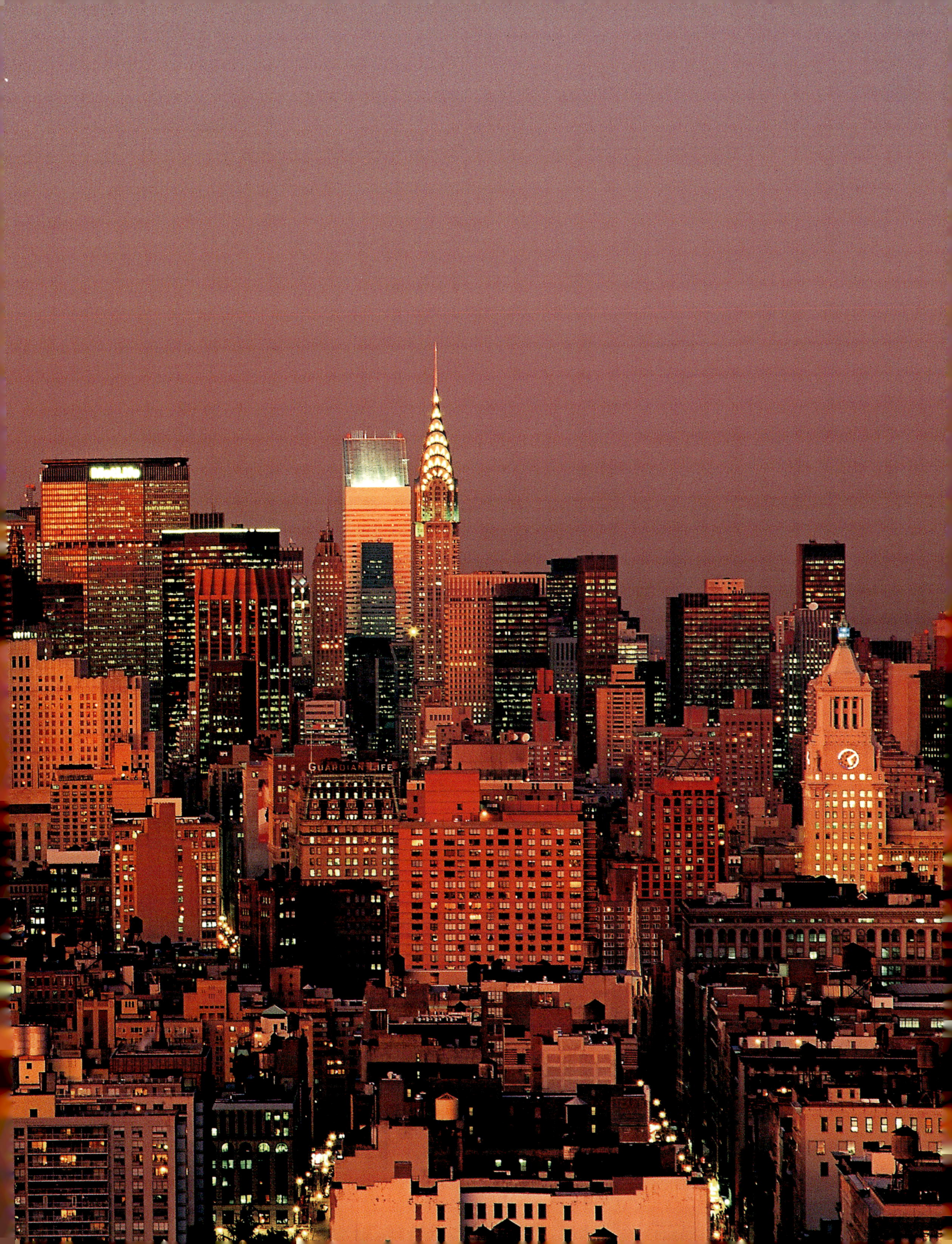
GUARDIAN LIFE

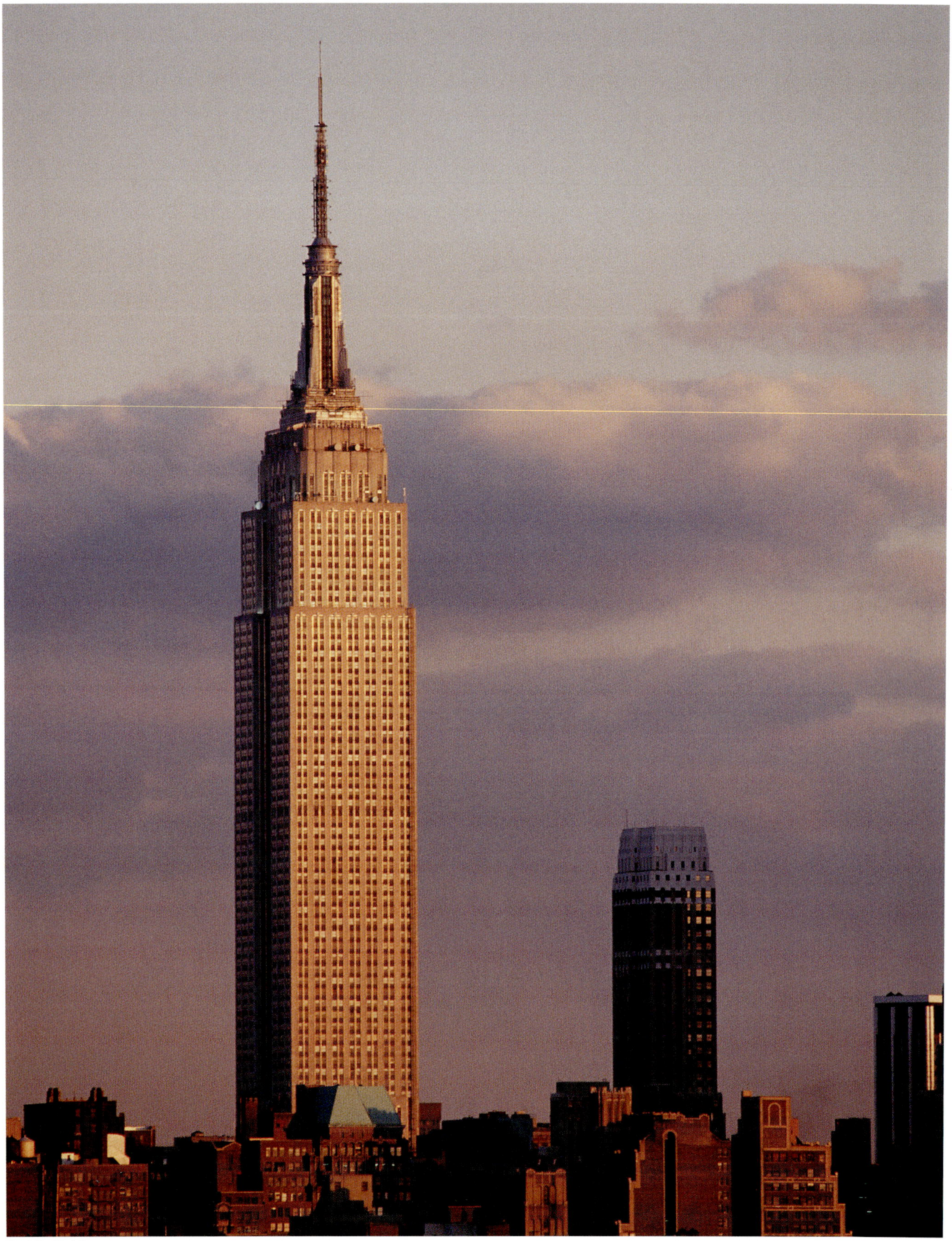

Photo © Patrick Batchelder

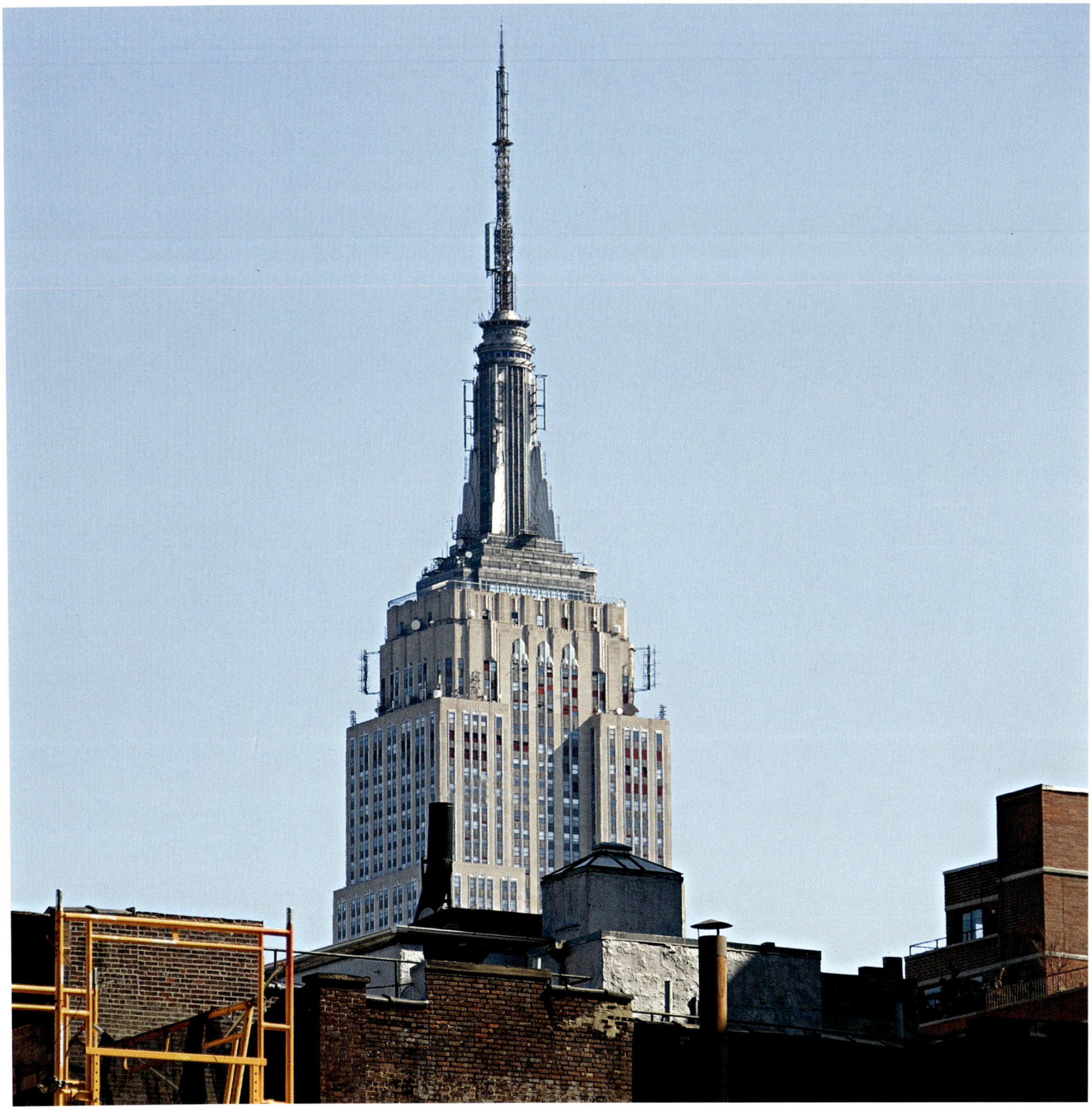

Photo by Joe Luman © Terrell Creative

LEFT: Looking east the Empire State Building basks in the warm light of the setting sun. The Nelson Tower, in front and to the right of the Empire State Building, which was also completed in 1931, is 46 stories tall.

ABOVE: Only the top 40 floors are visible from this vantage point near Chelsea Market.

FOLLOWING PAGES: A full moon shines above Midtown, over Times Square. The Empire State Building, lit in its traditional white/white/white configuration stands 1,454 feet tall on the right.

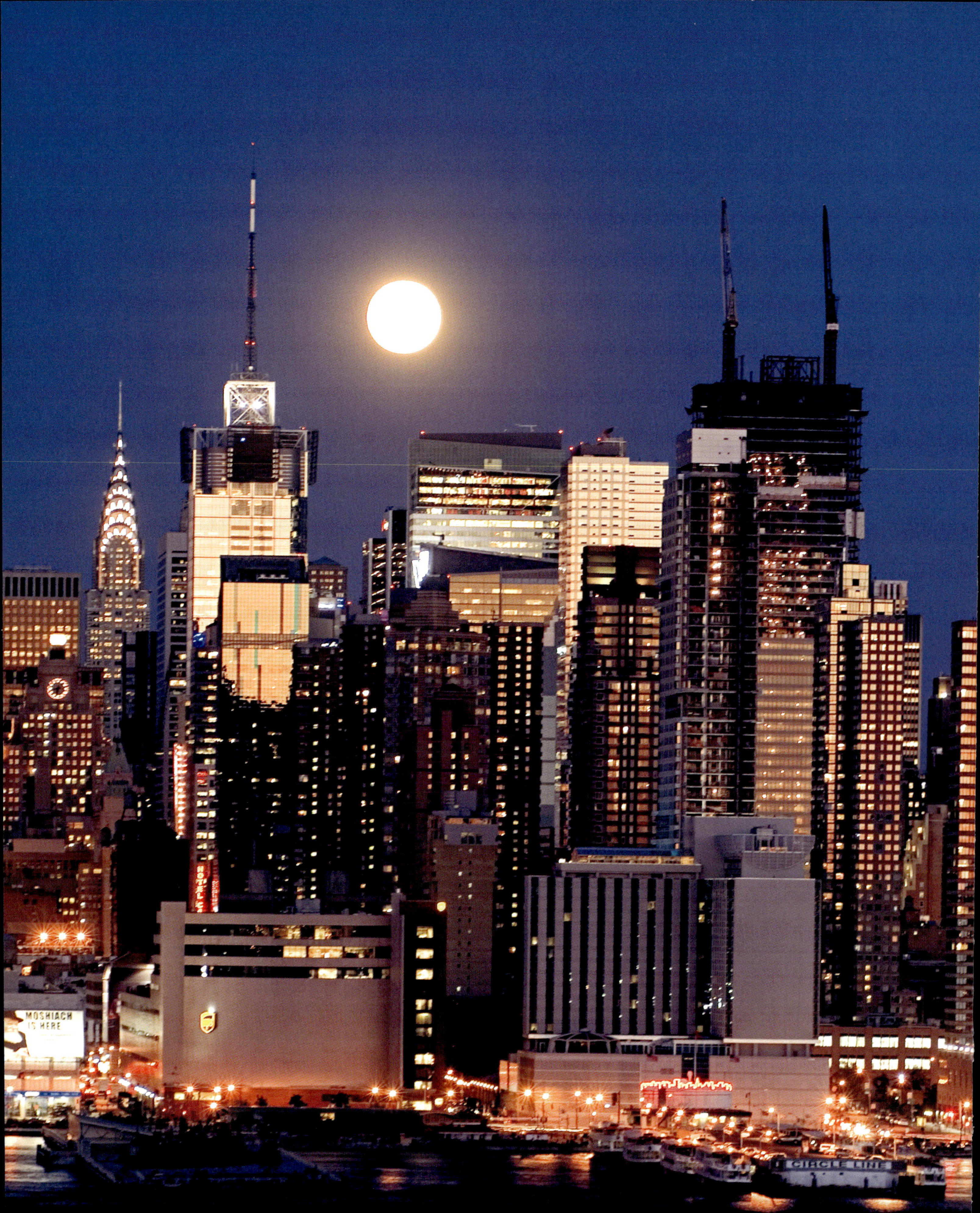
MOSHIACH
IS HERE
CIRCLE LINE

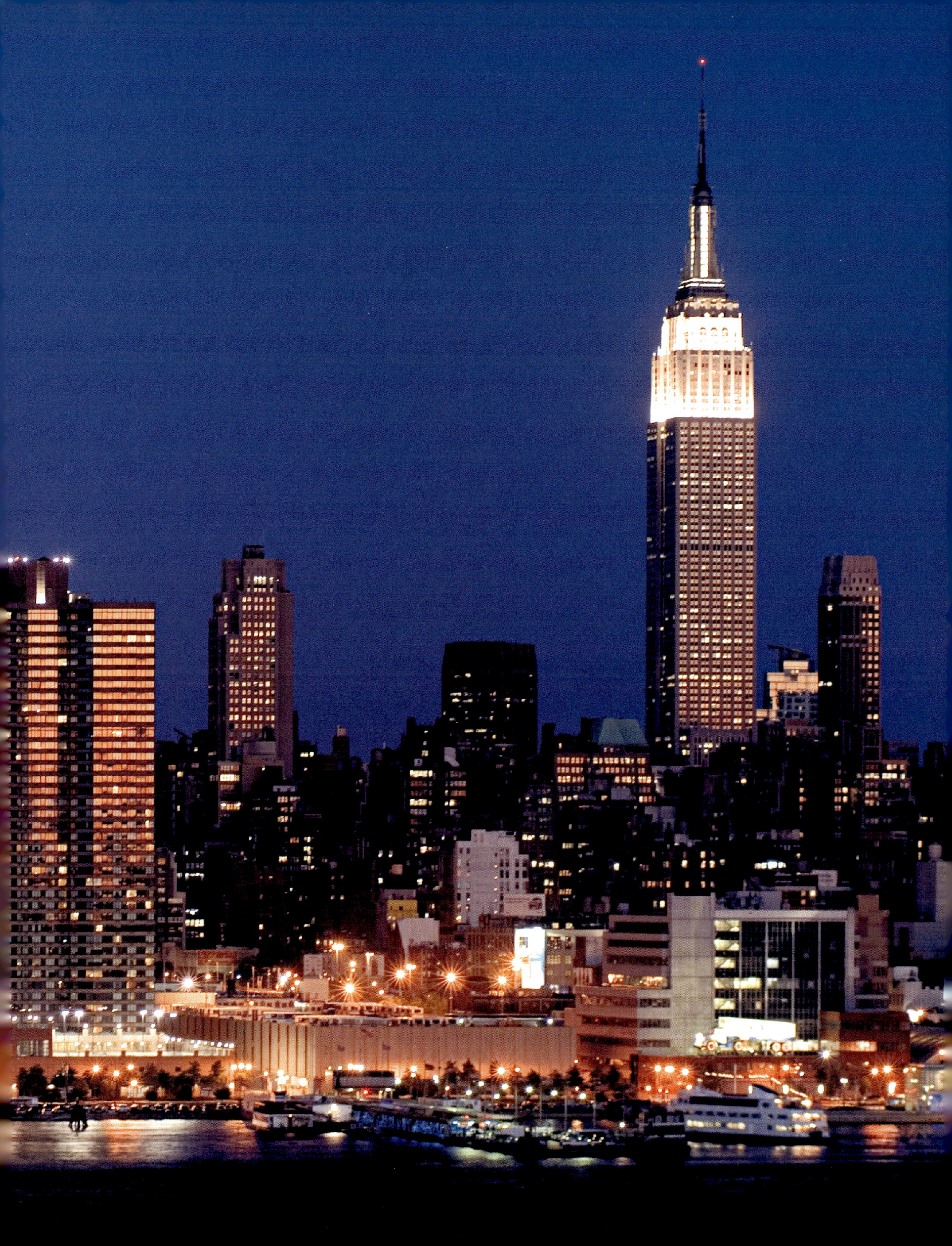

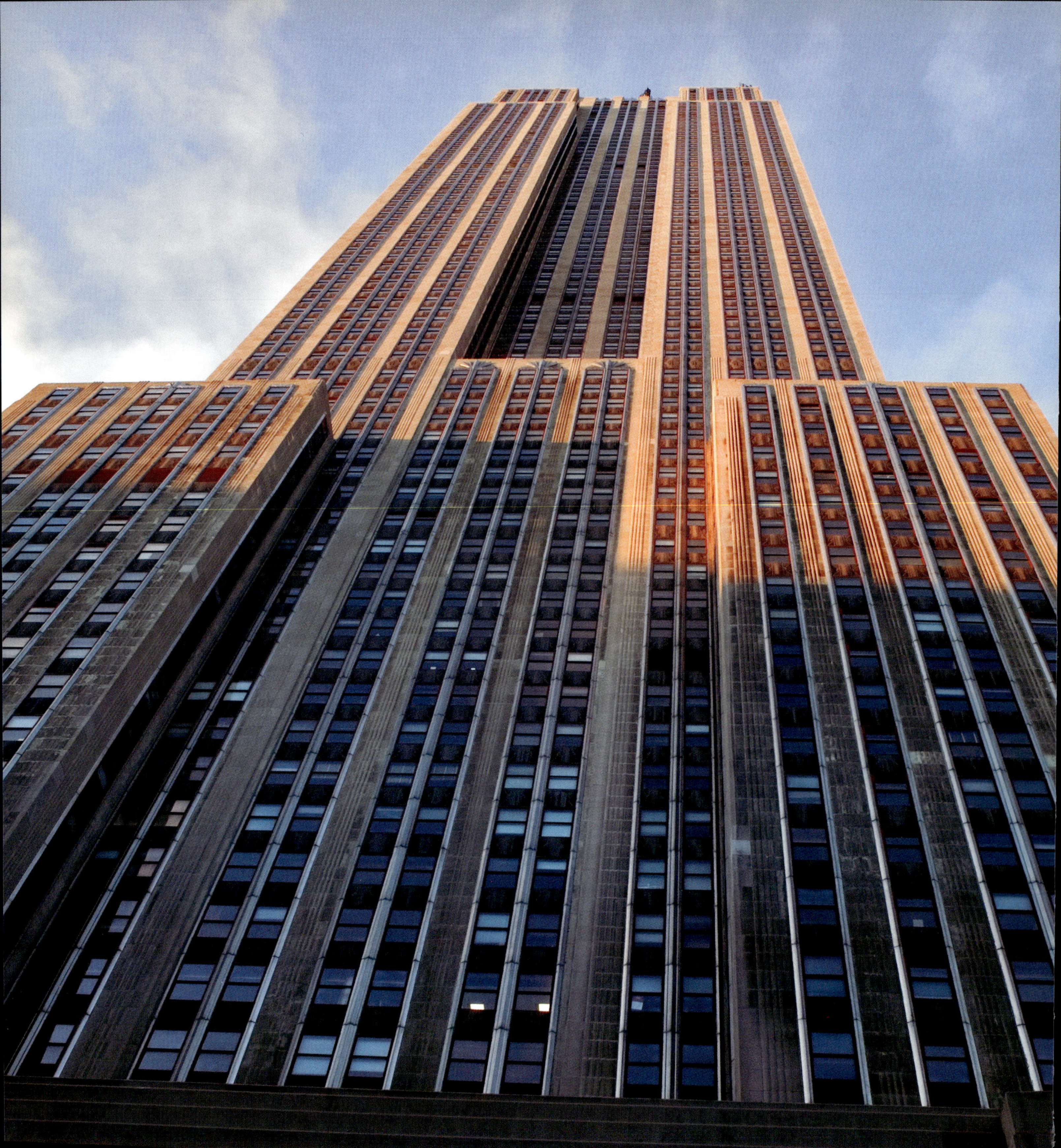

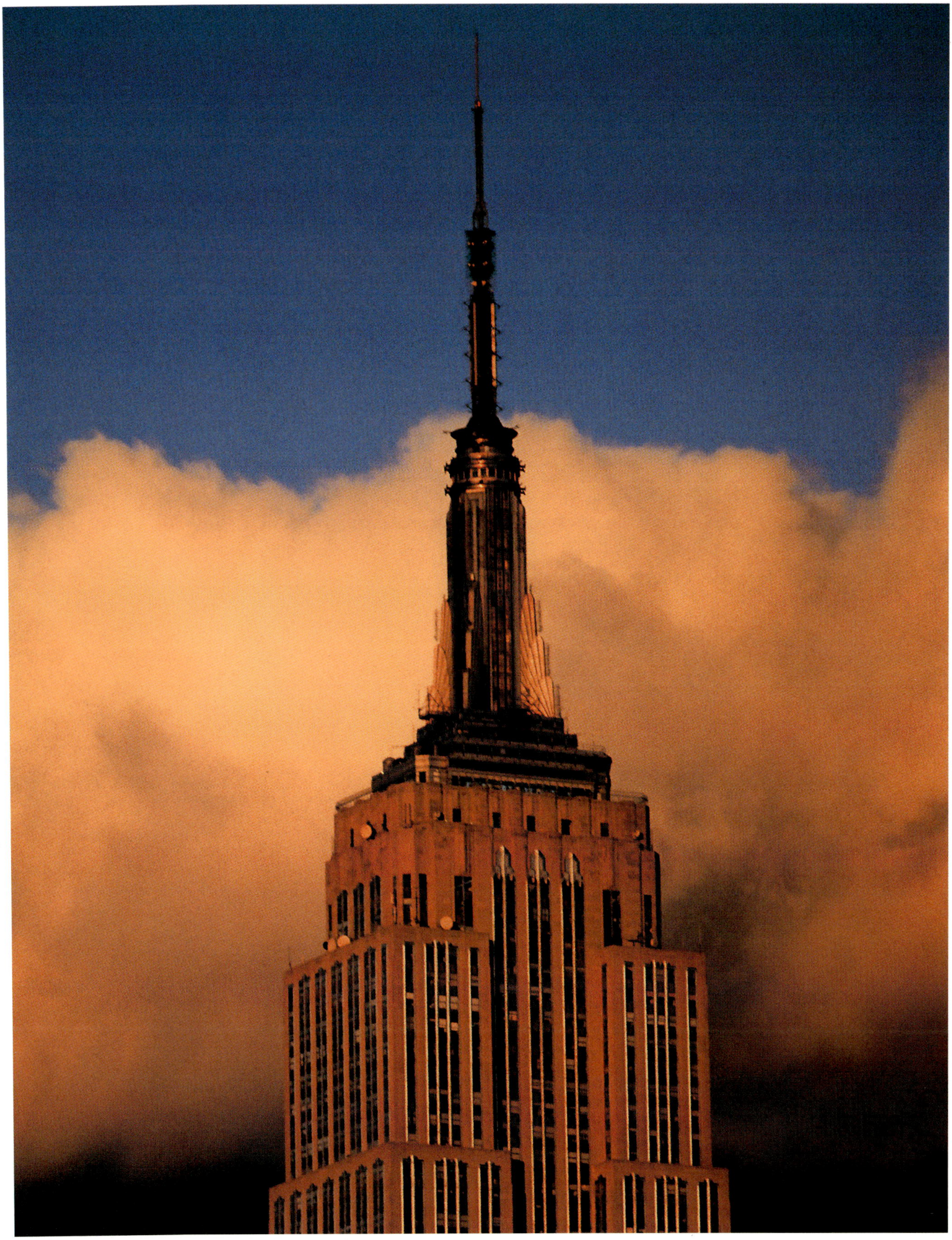

Photo © Grace Davies

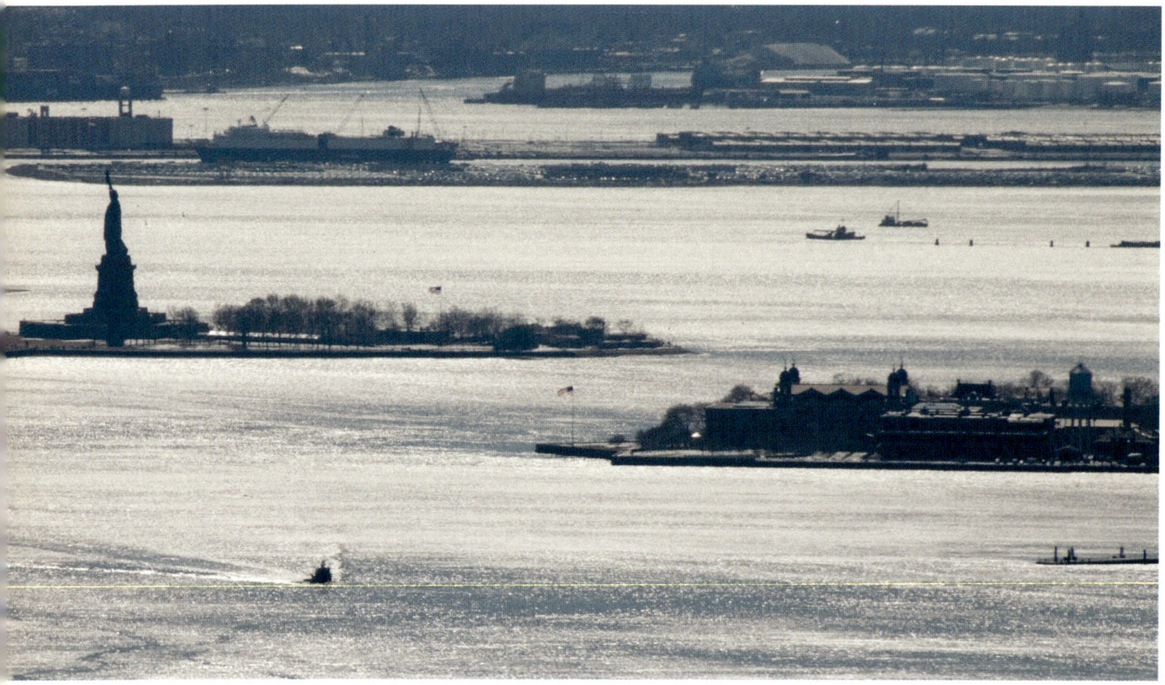

Photo by Joe Luman © Terrell Creative

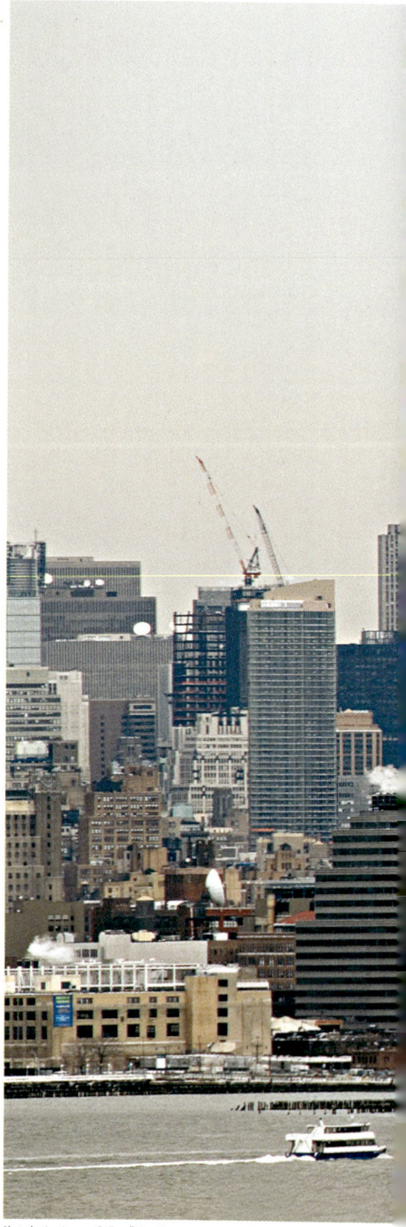

Photo by Joe Luman © Terrell Creative

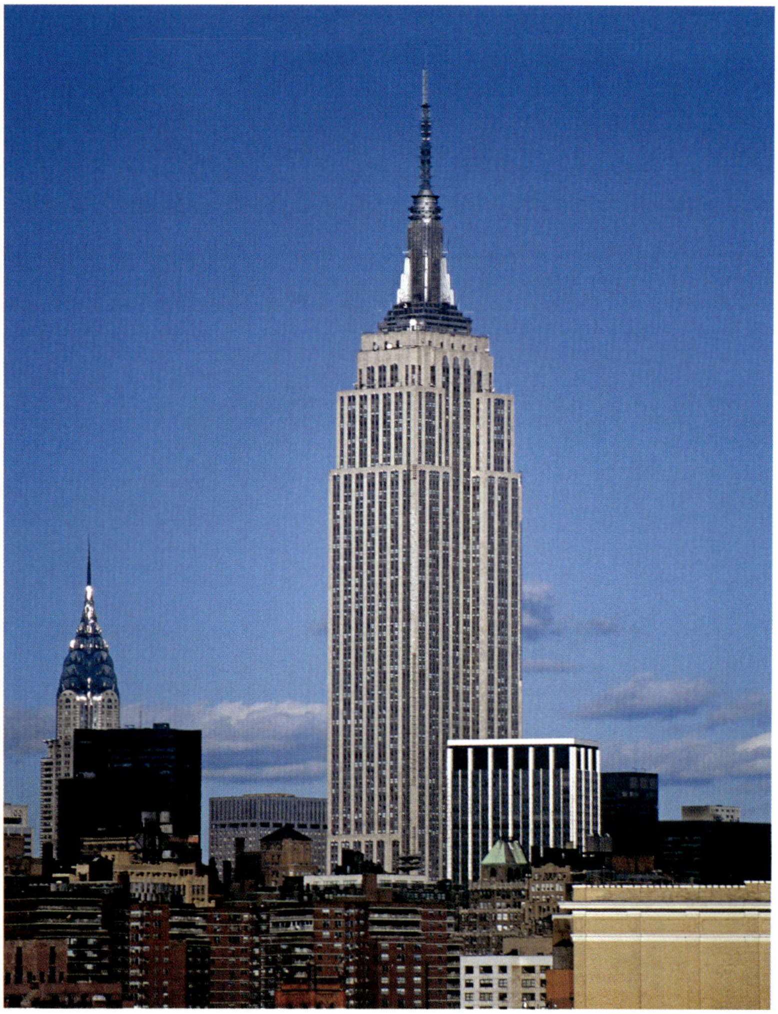

Photo © Lynn Seldon

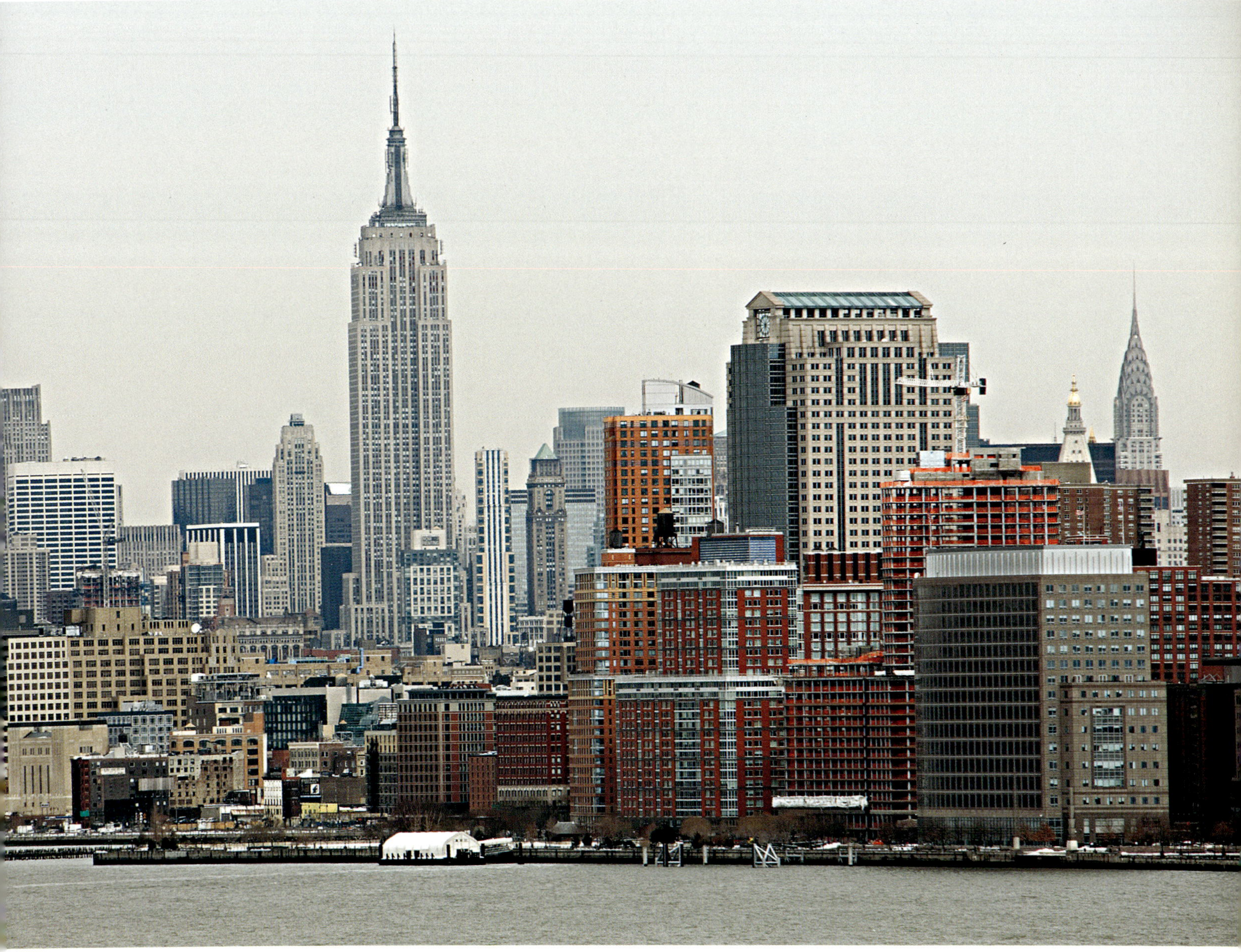

PREVIOUS PAGES, LEFT: The morning sun highlights the top half of the Empire State Building in this photo taken across 34th Street, looking nearly straight up. **RIGHT:** The 86th Floor Observatory as well as the windows of the 102nd Floor Observatory are clearly visible in this close-up view of the top the Empire State Building.

TOP LEFT: From the 86th floor the telephoto lens captures this view of the Statue of Liberty and Ellis Island in New York Harbor. **BOTTOM LEFT:** The once-tallest Chrysler Building looks small when compared with the Empire State Building in this photo looking to the northeast. **ABOVE:** This view of the Empire State Building was taken from the observation deck of the Statue of Liberty.

FOLLOWING PAGES: The rising sun casts a warm glow on the Manhattan skyline fronting the East River in this aerial image.

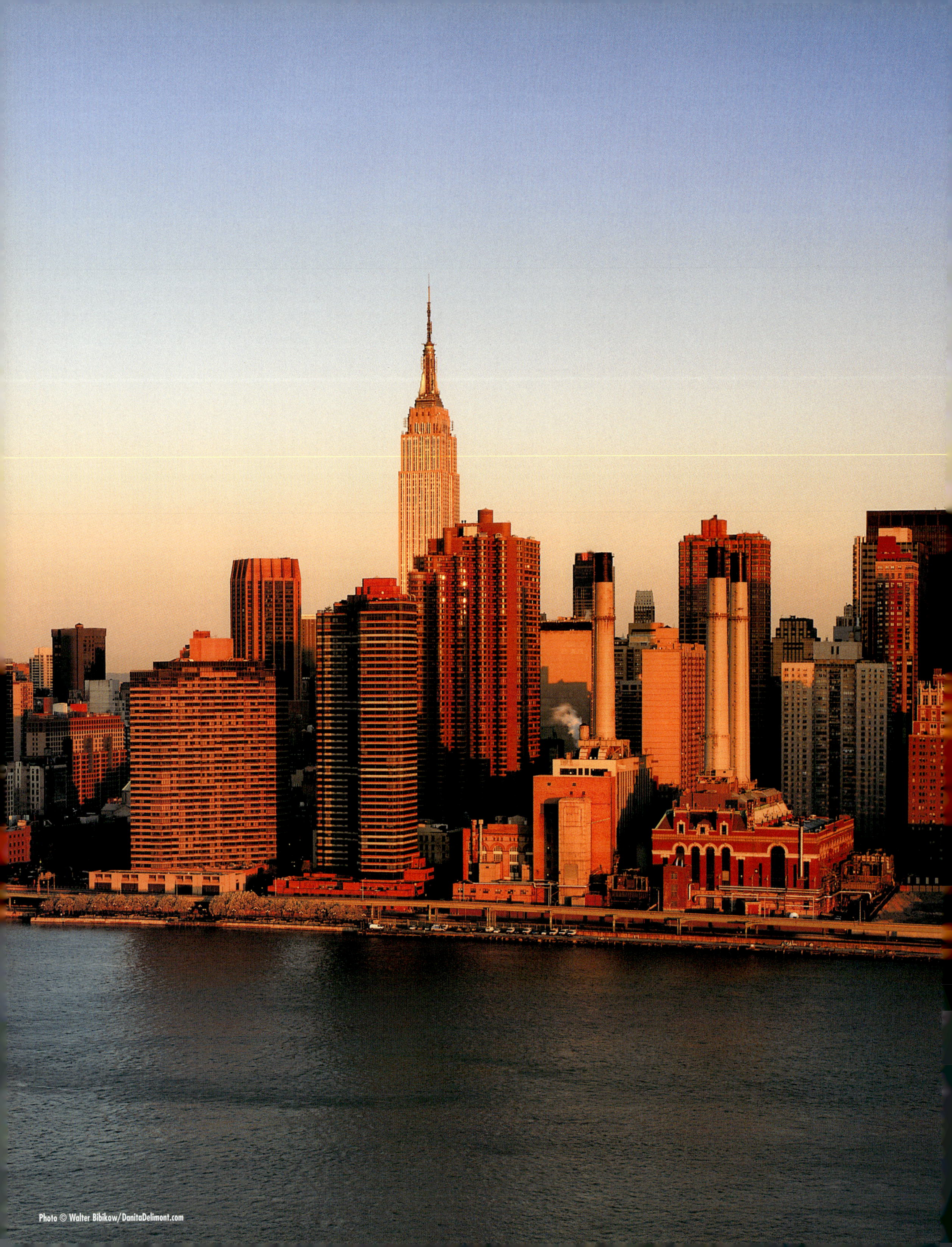

Photo © Walter Bibikow/DanitaDelimont.com

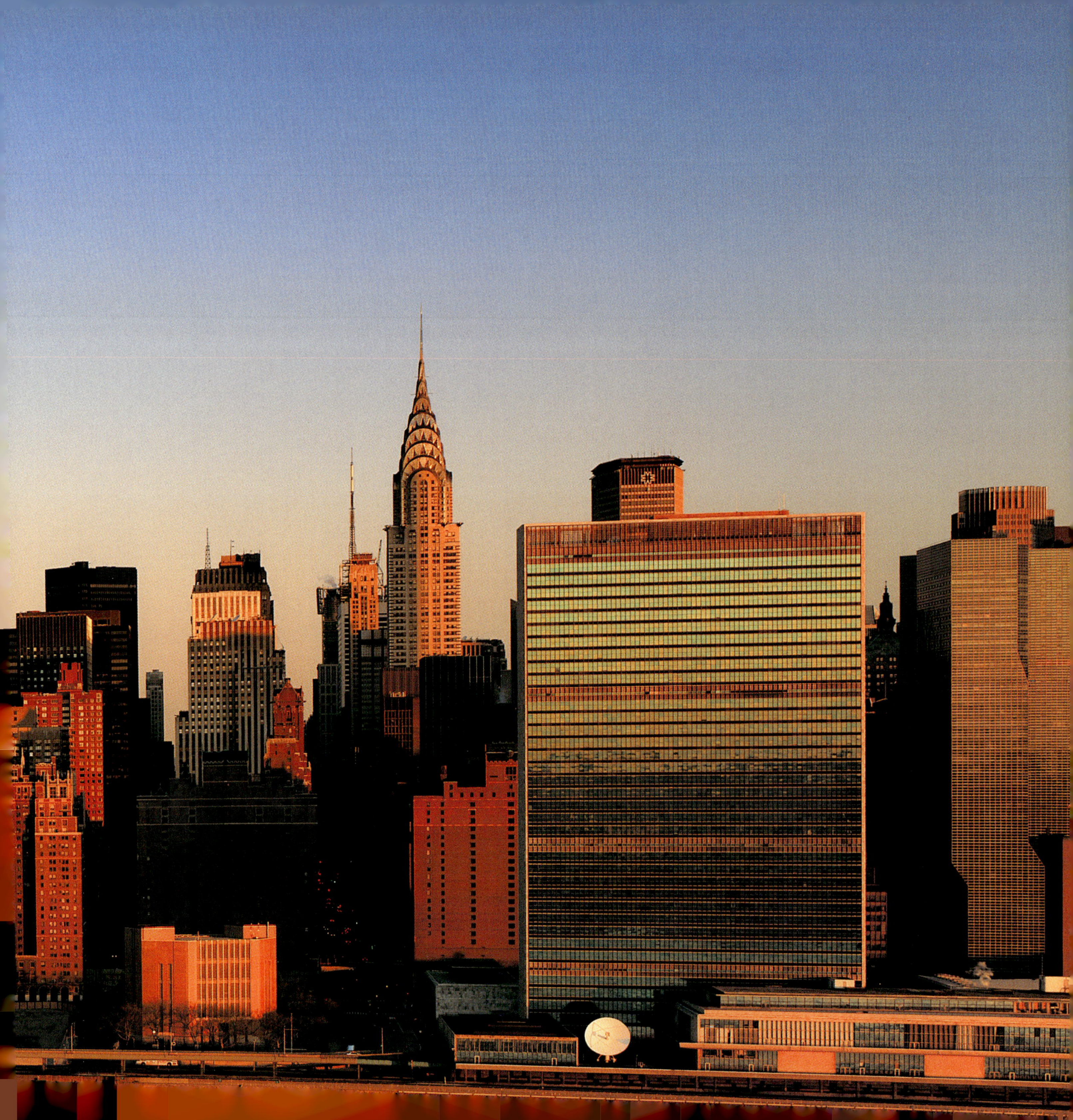

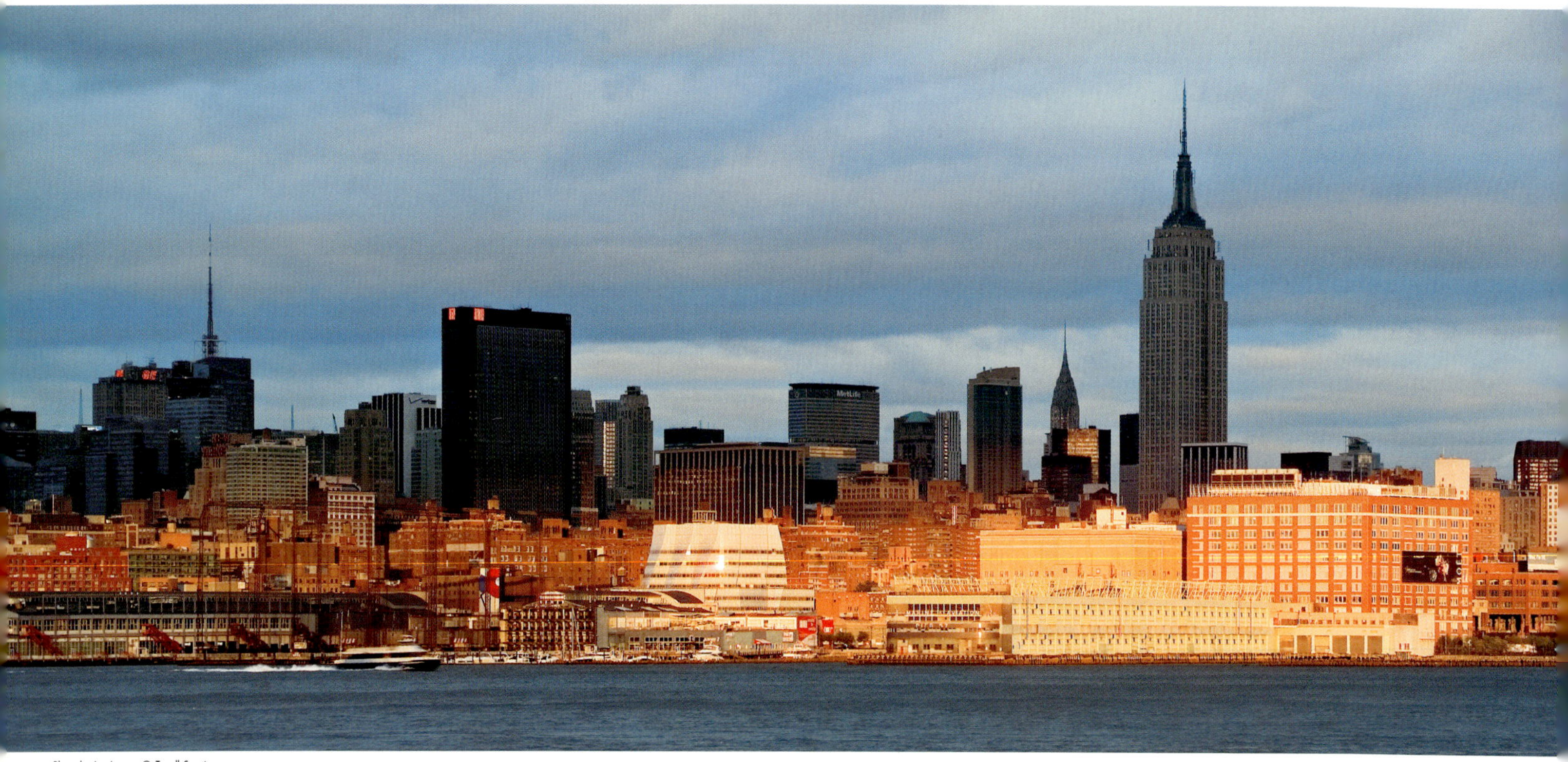

Photo by Joe Luman © Terrell Creative

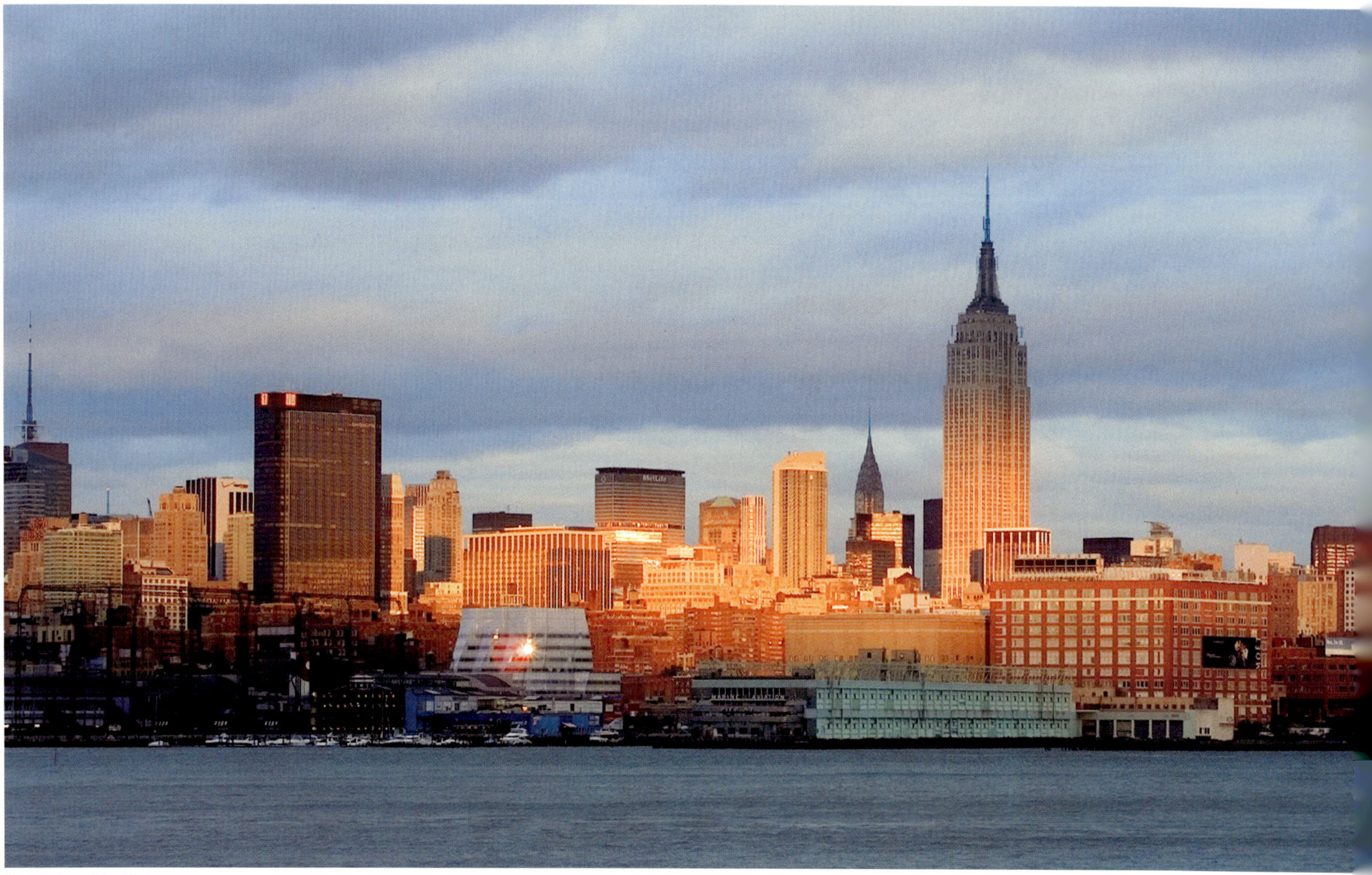

Photo by Joe Luman © Terrell Creative

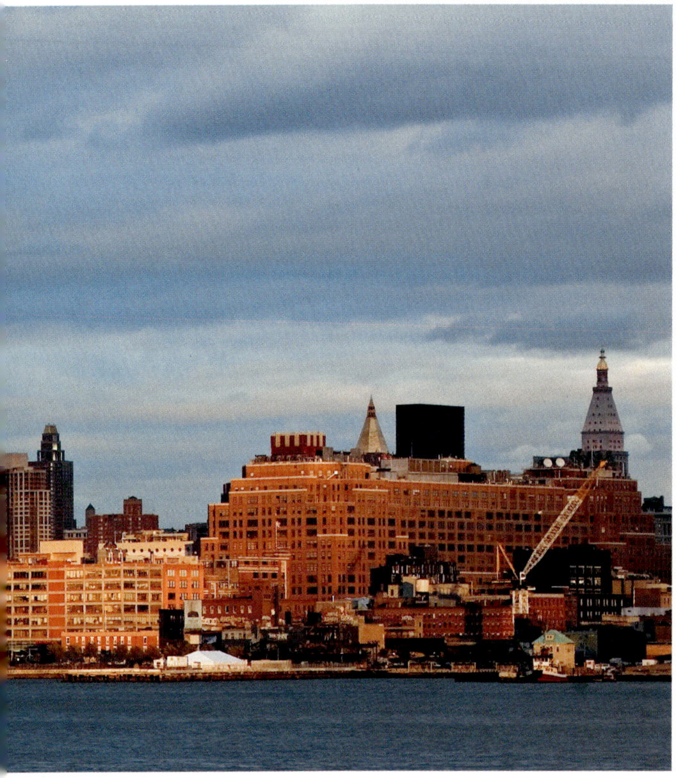

LEFT: A cloudy day in New York City gives way to a small crack in the clouds, allowing a small area of sunlight to shine on a few buildings on the Hudson River. **BELOW LEFT:** The area of sunlight begins to move eastward illuminating the lower half of the Empire State Building. **BELOW RIGHT:** Finally the sunlight brightens all of the Empire State Building up to the 86th Floor Observatory. This was as far east as this area of sunlight moved, and in a few seconds after this photo, the sky closed and a blanket of clouds again covered all of Manhattan.

FOLLOWING PAGES: The sky to the southwest still retains the red glow after sunset as dark settles in over the city. The lights of automobiles on 6th Avenue stream southward toward the financial district, past the World Trade Center site. The Statue of Liberty is visible in New York Harbor on the right, while the lights on the Brooklyn Bridge mark the span across the East River. The green lights of the Verrazano-Narrows Bridge are in the distance.

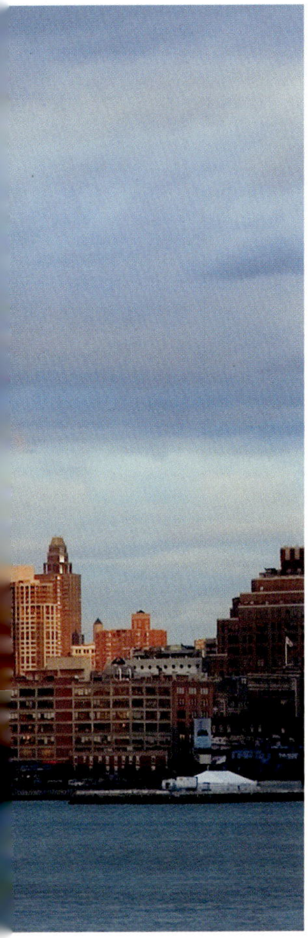

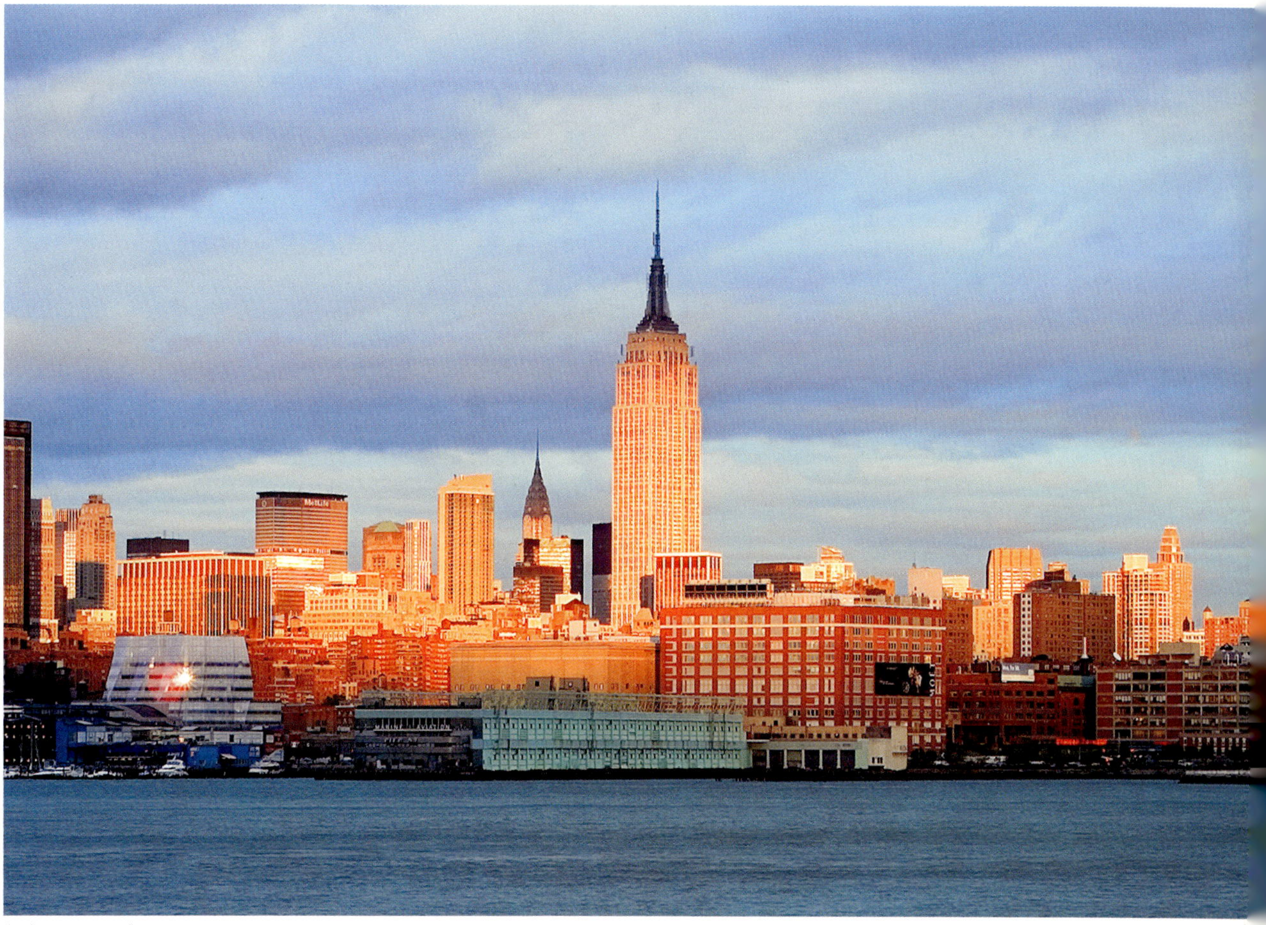

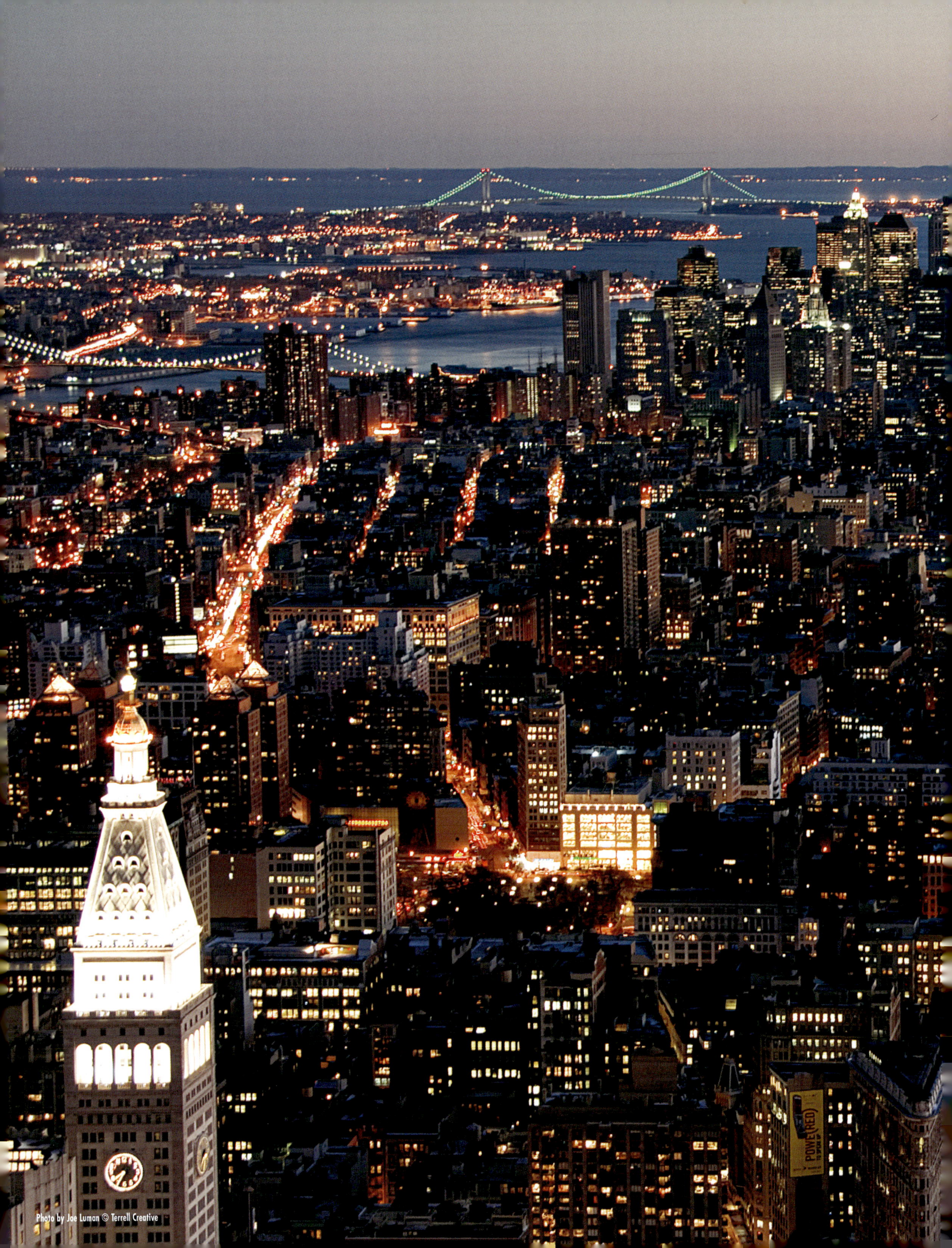
Photo by Joe Luman © Terrell Creative

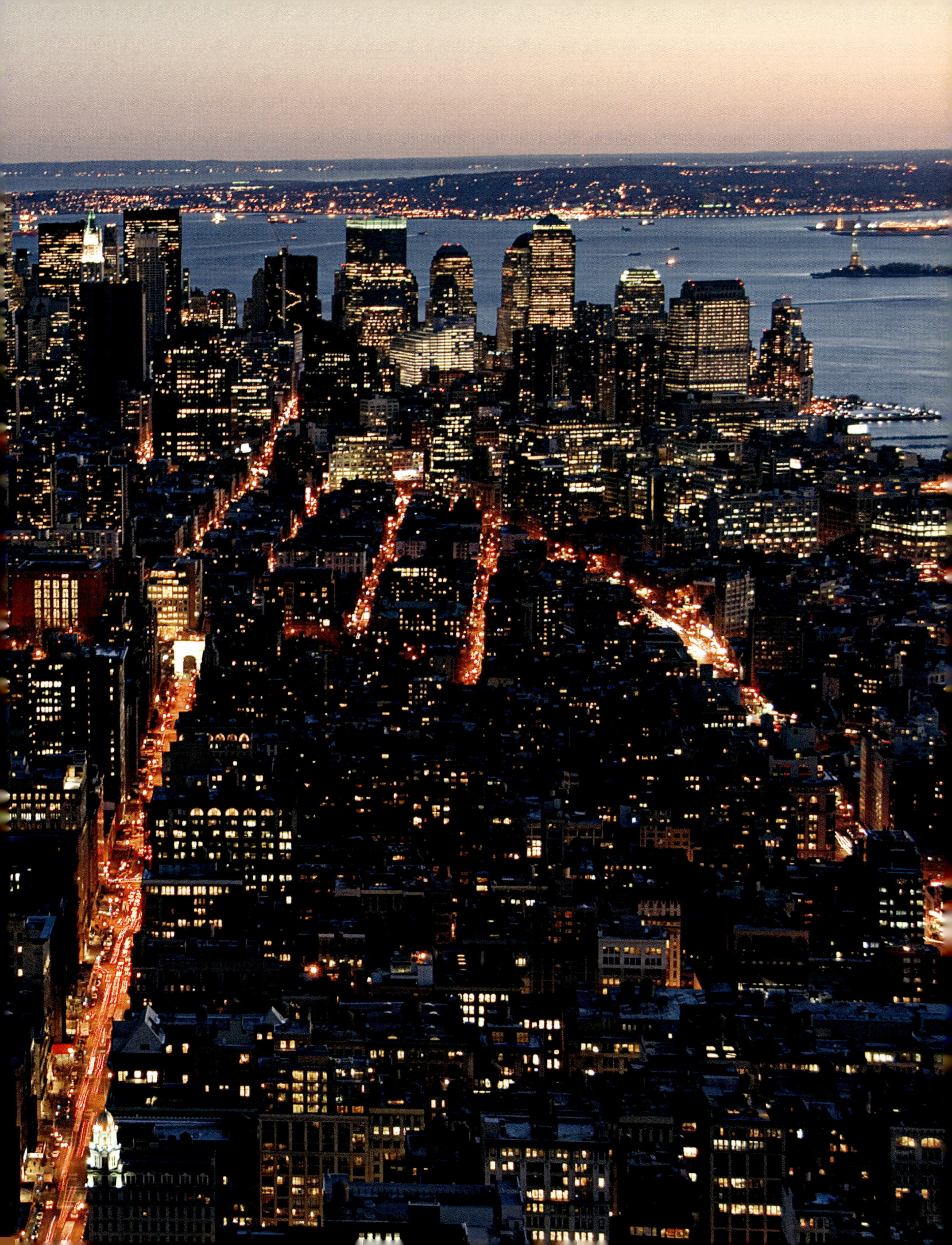

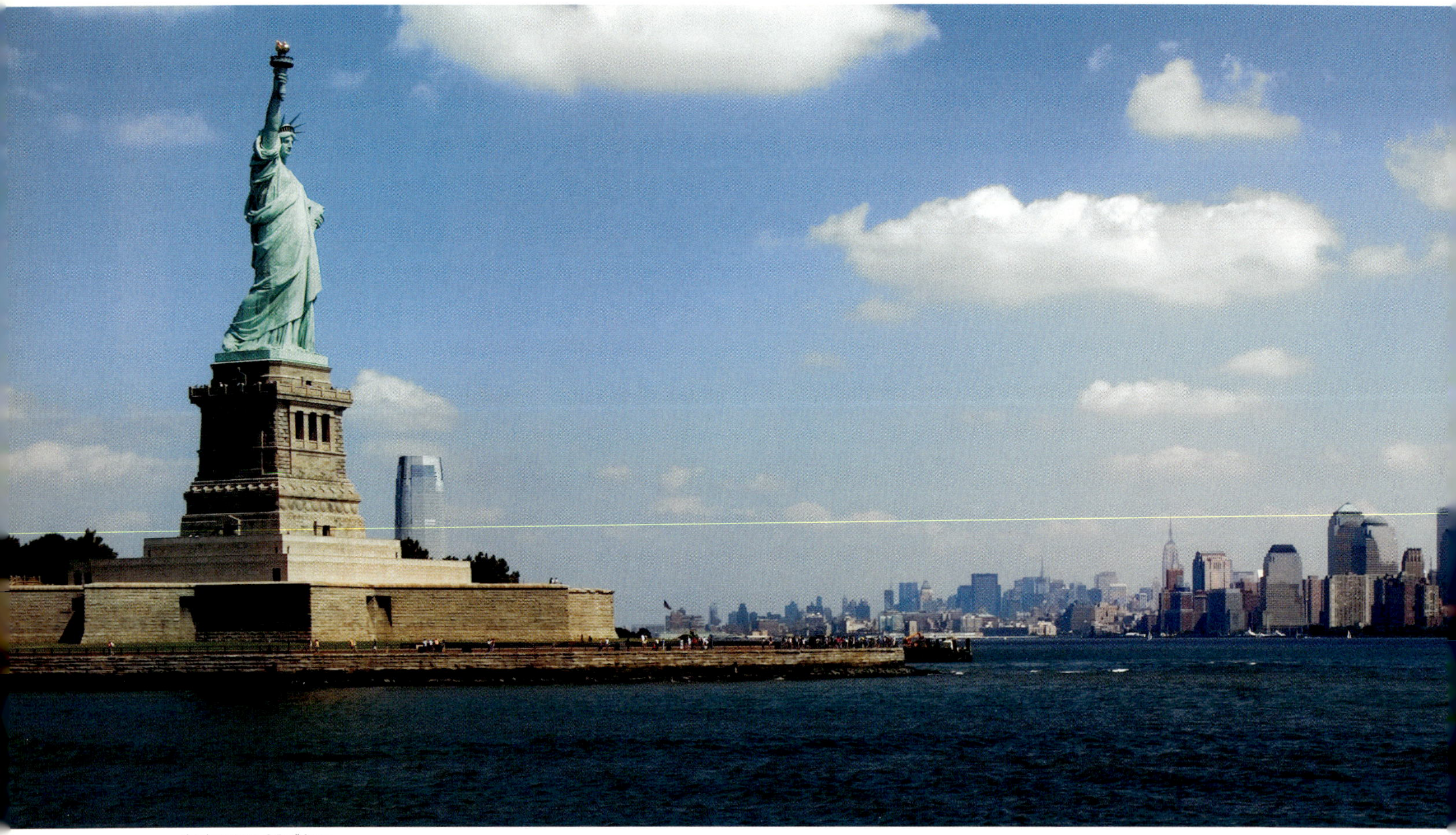

Photo by Joe Luman © Terrell Creative

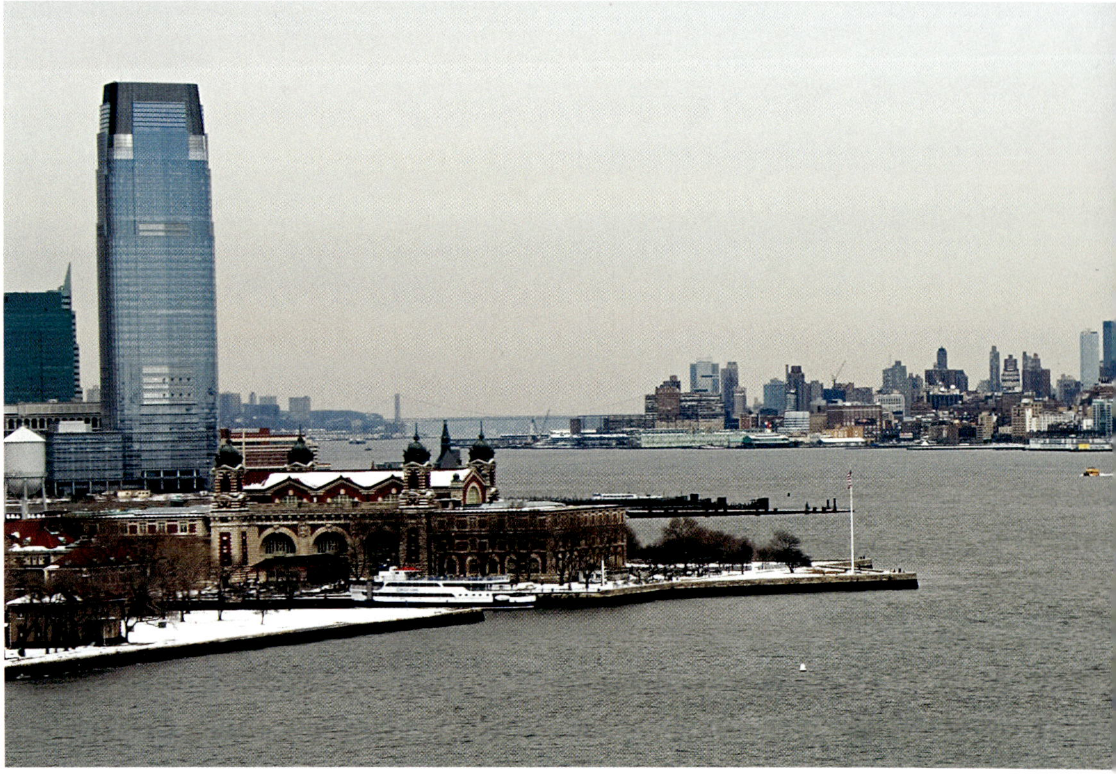

Photo by Joe Luman © Terrell Creative

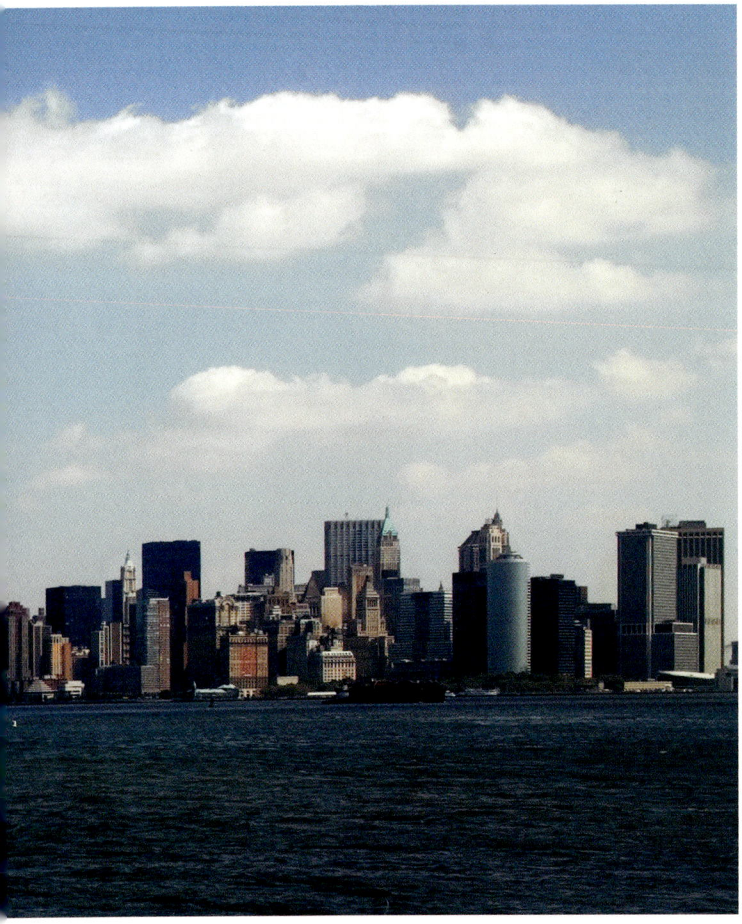

LEFT: Lady Liberty welcomes ships arriving to New York Harbor in this photo taken from the Circle Line Ferry to Liberty Island.

BELOW: This view from the observation deck of the Statue of Liberty shows from left to right, Ellis Island, Goldman Sachs Tower, the tallest building in New Jersey at 781 feet tall, and the Hudson River. On the right in the background is the Woolworth Building, in 1913 the world's tallest building at 792 feet. At the center of the photo is the Empire State Building.

FOLLOWING PAGES: The Empire State Building sparkles like the jewel that it is in the early evening sunlight in this aerial photo taken over the Hudson River.

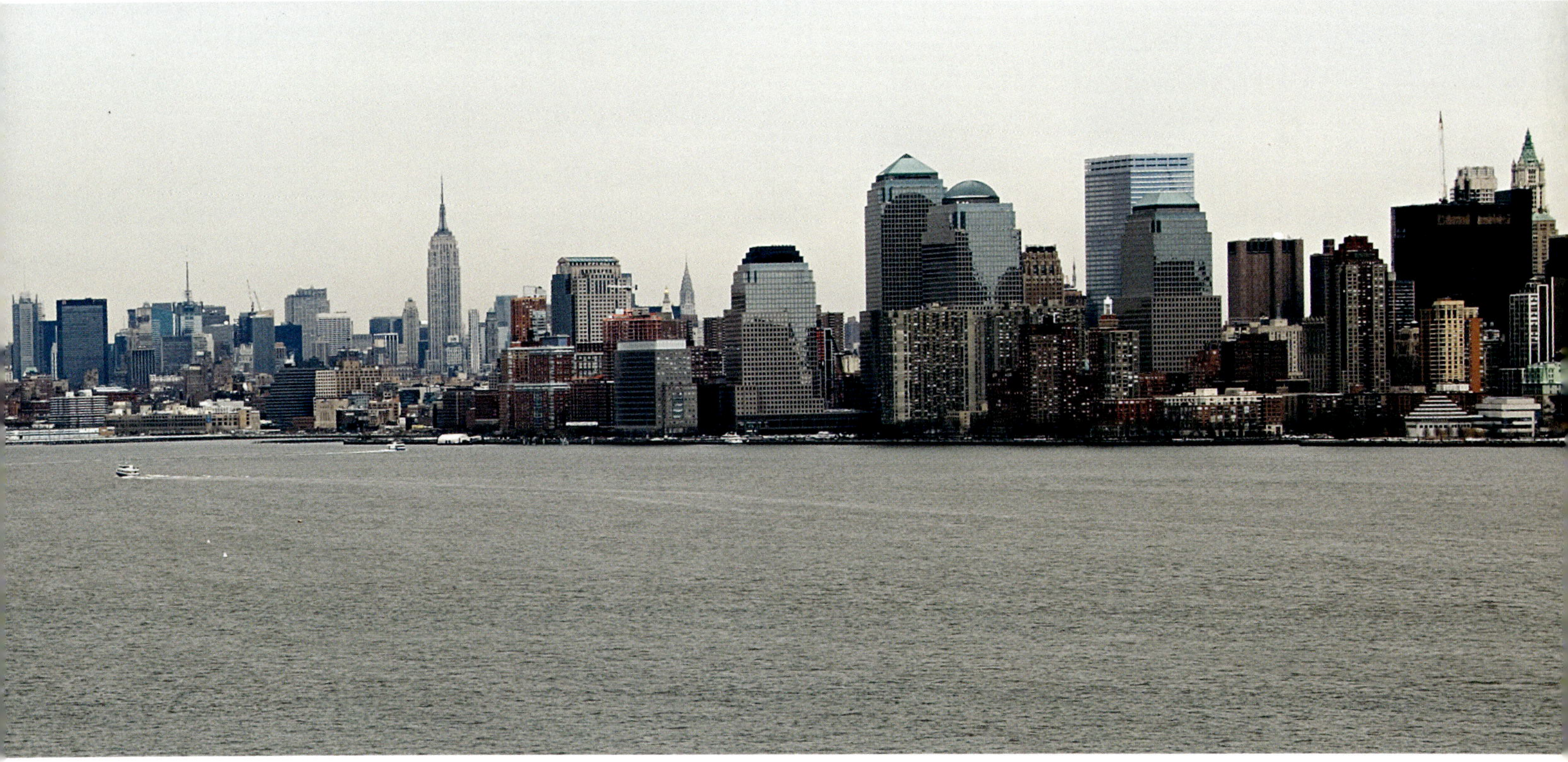

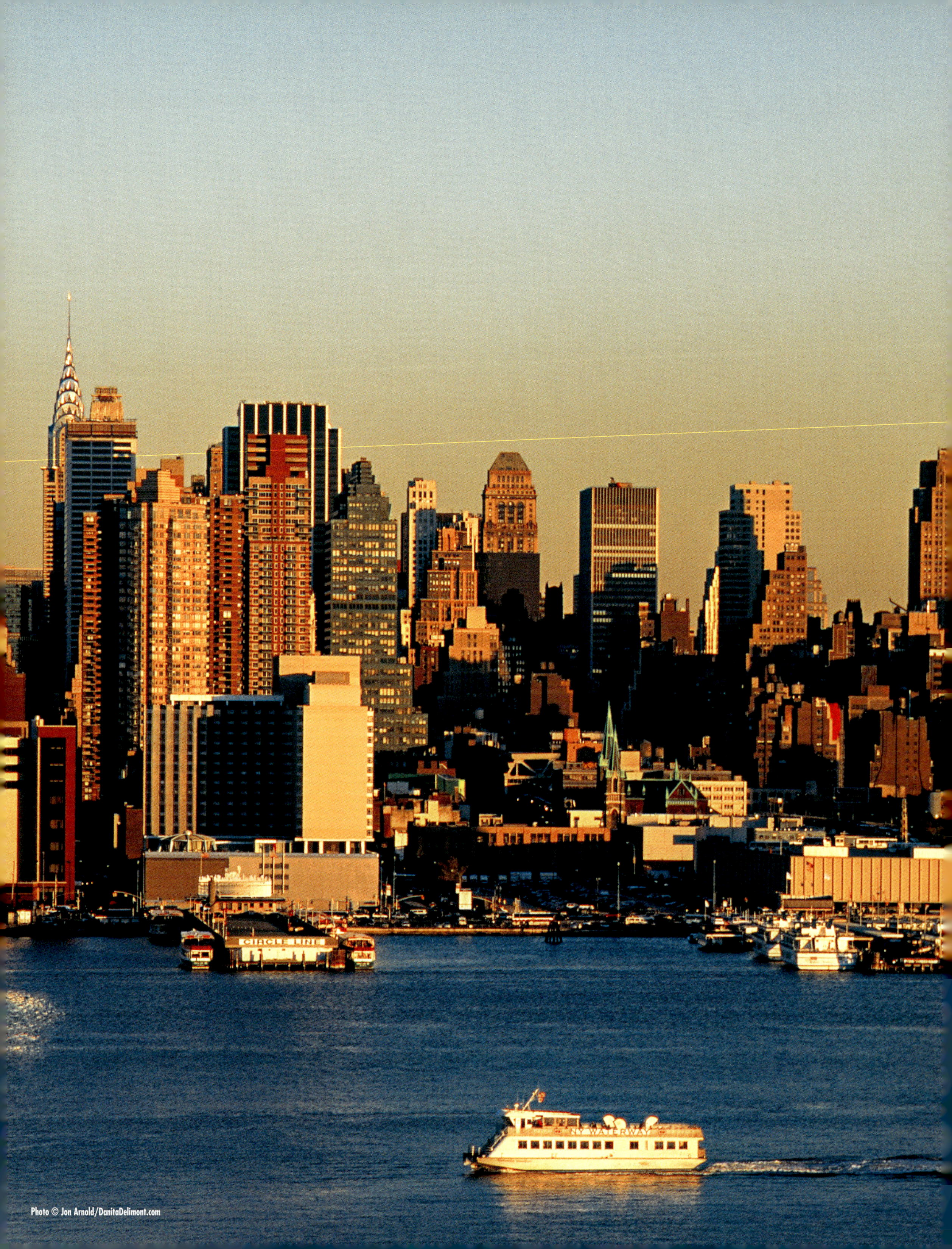

Photo © Jon Arnold/DanitaDelimont.com

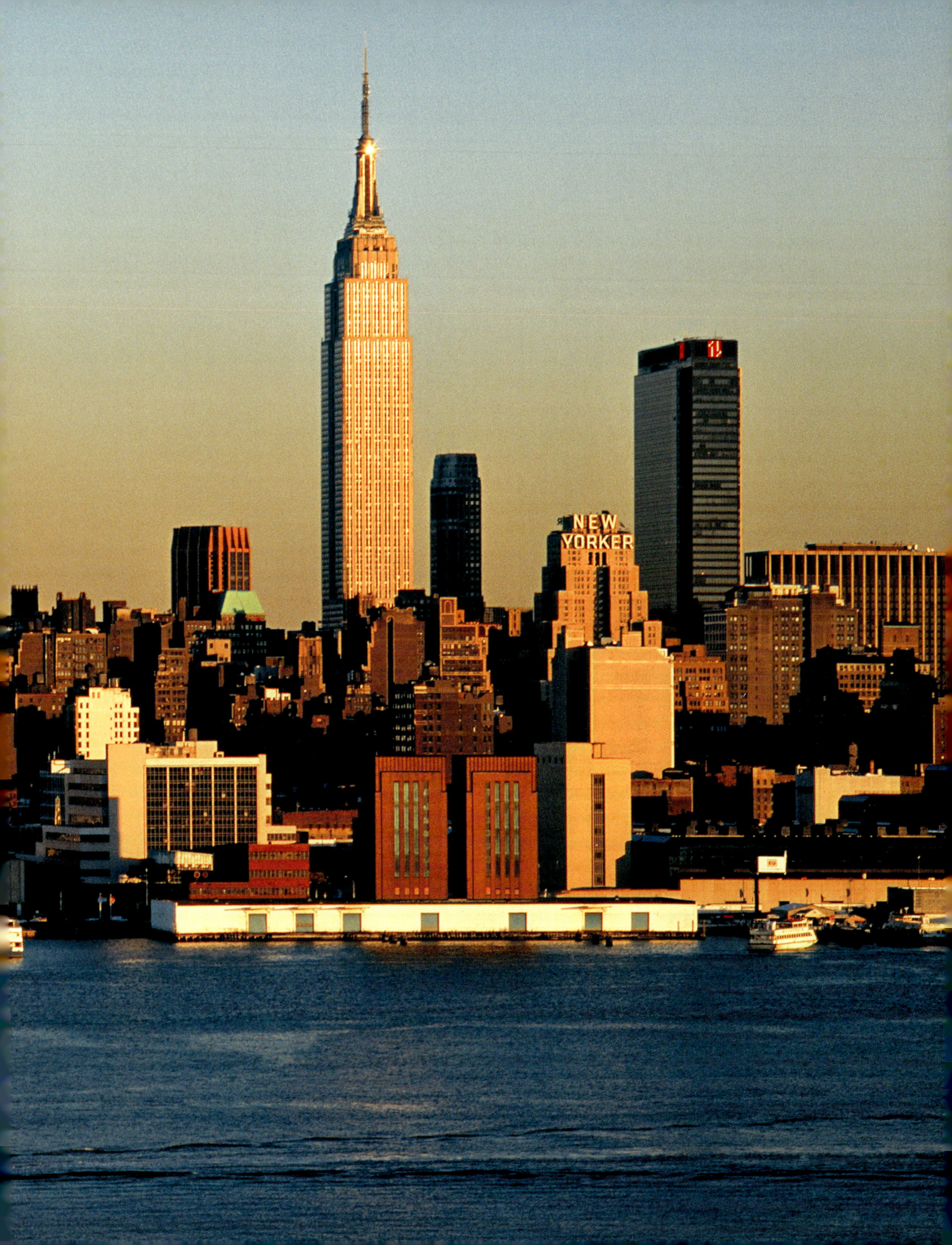
NEW
YORKER

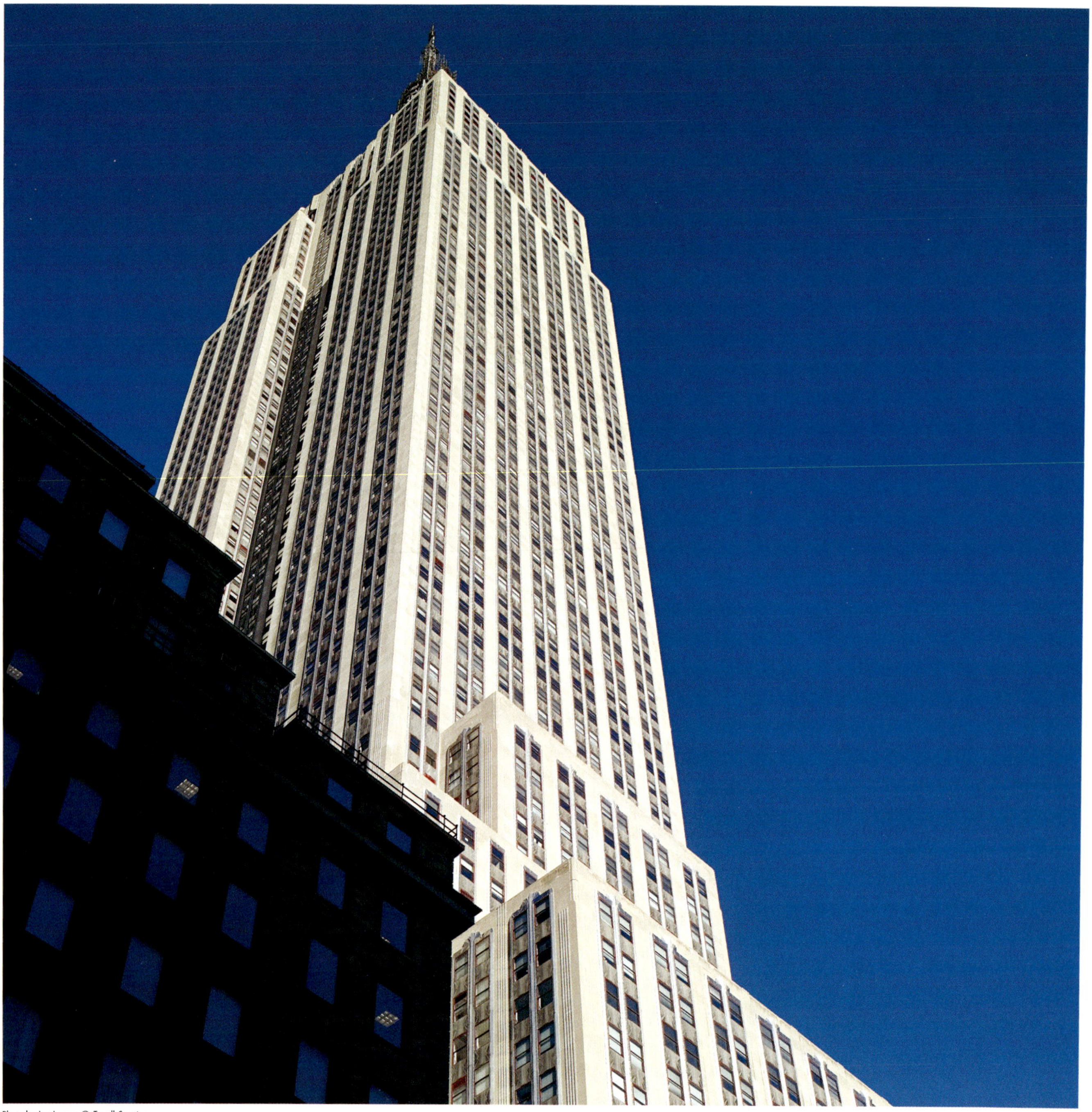

Photo by Joe Luman © Terrell Creative

ABOVE: The blue sky forms a great contrast to the sunbathed Empire State Building. **RIGHT:** Pictured here is the 33rd Street view of the Empire State Building from Herald Square.

FOLLOWING PAGES: This classic wide-angle image of Midtown and Uptown Manhattan clearly shows how dominating the Empire State Building is over the New York City skyline.

FINAL PAGE: The roof of the Market Center at 27th Street between Fifth Avenue and Broadway provides the vantage point for this magnificent photo of the south façade of the Empire State Building.

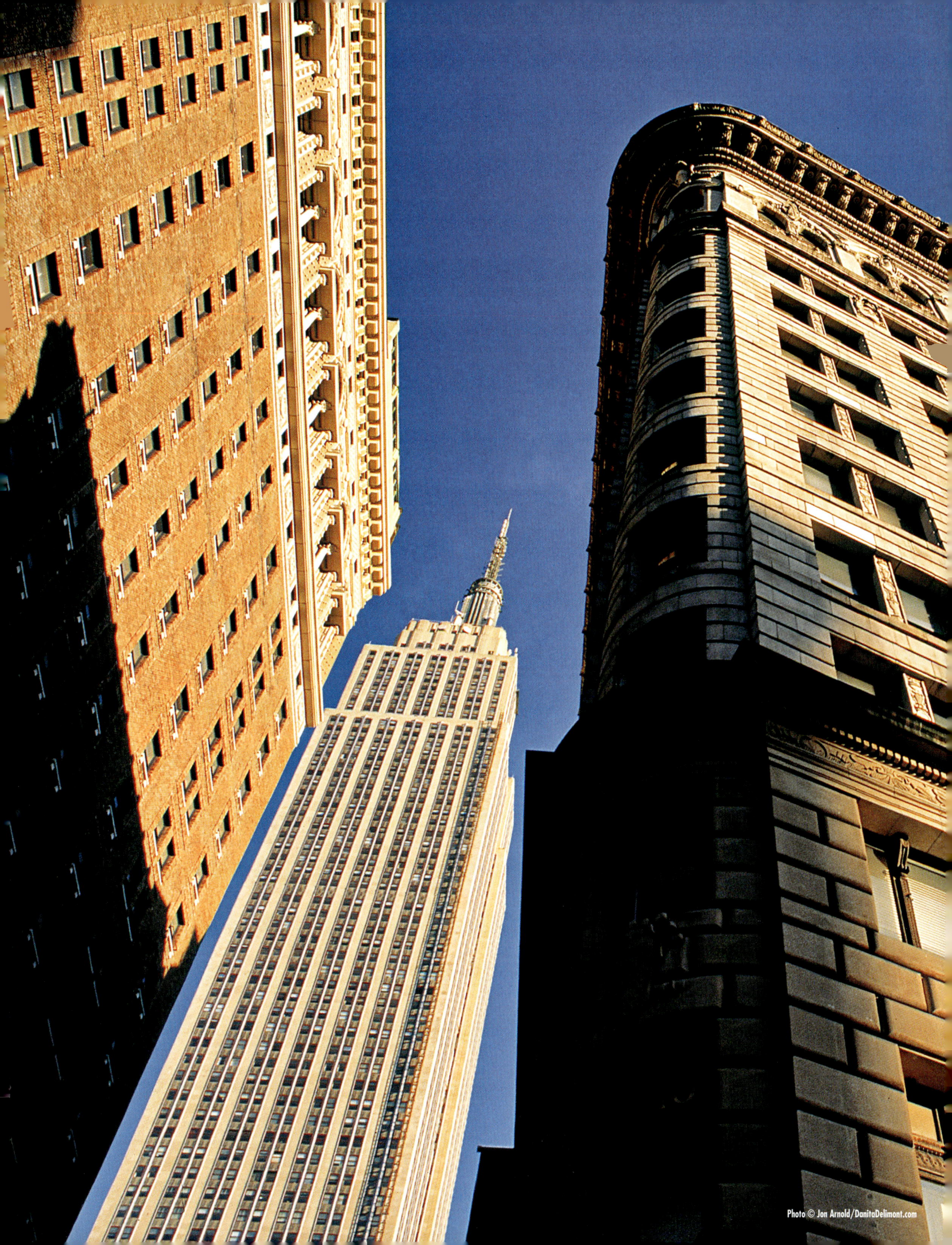
Photo © Jon Arnold/DanitaDelimont.com

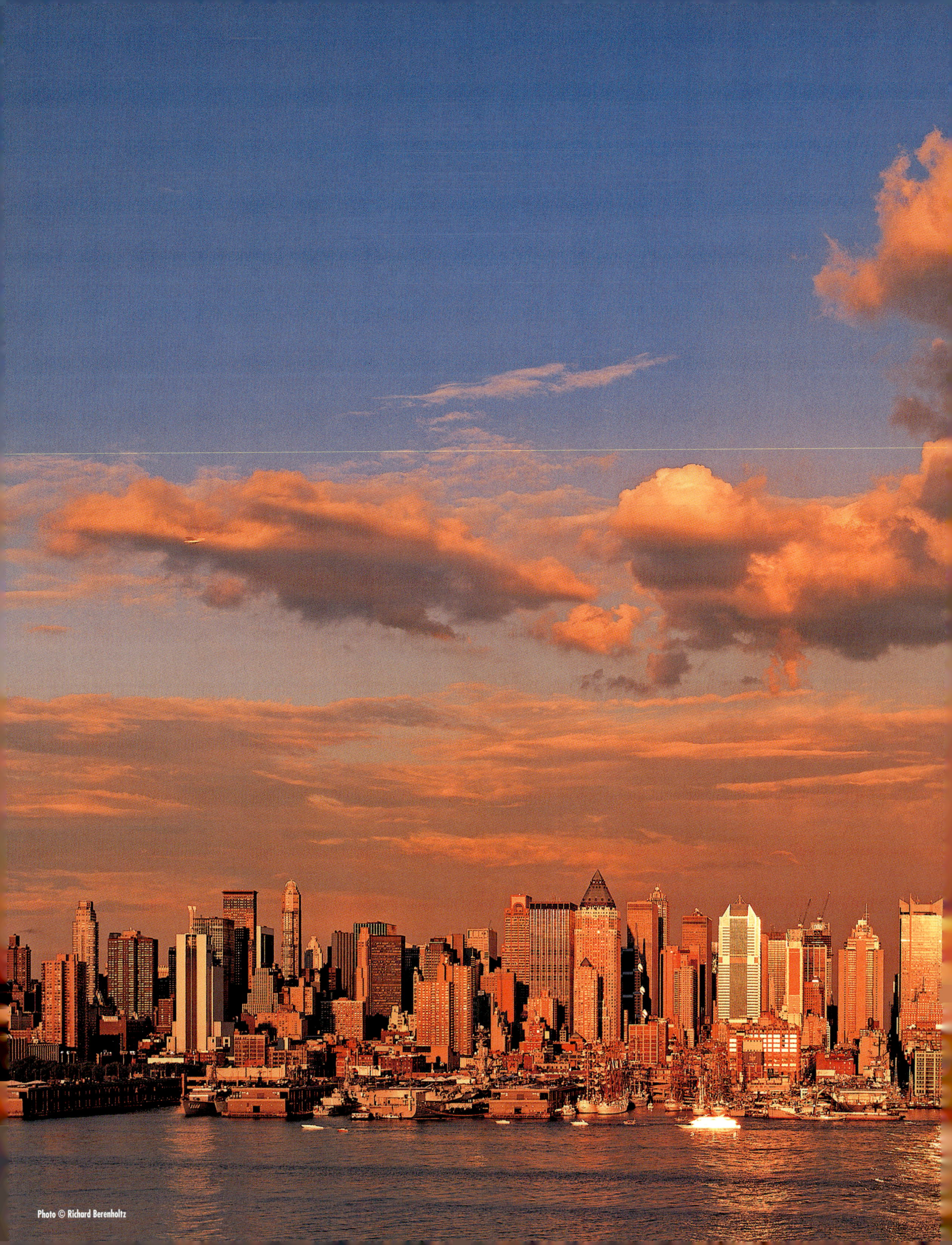

Photo © Richard Berenholtz

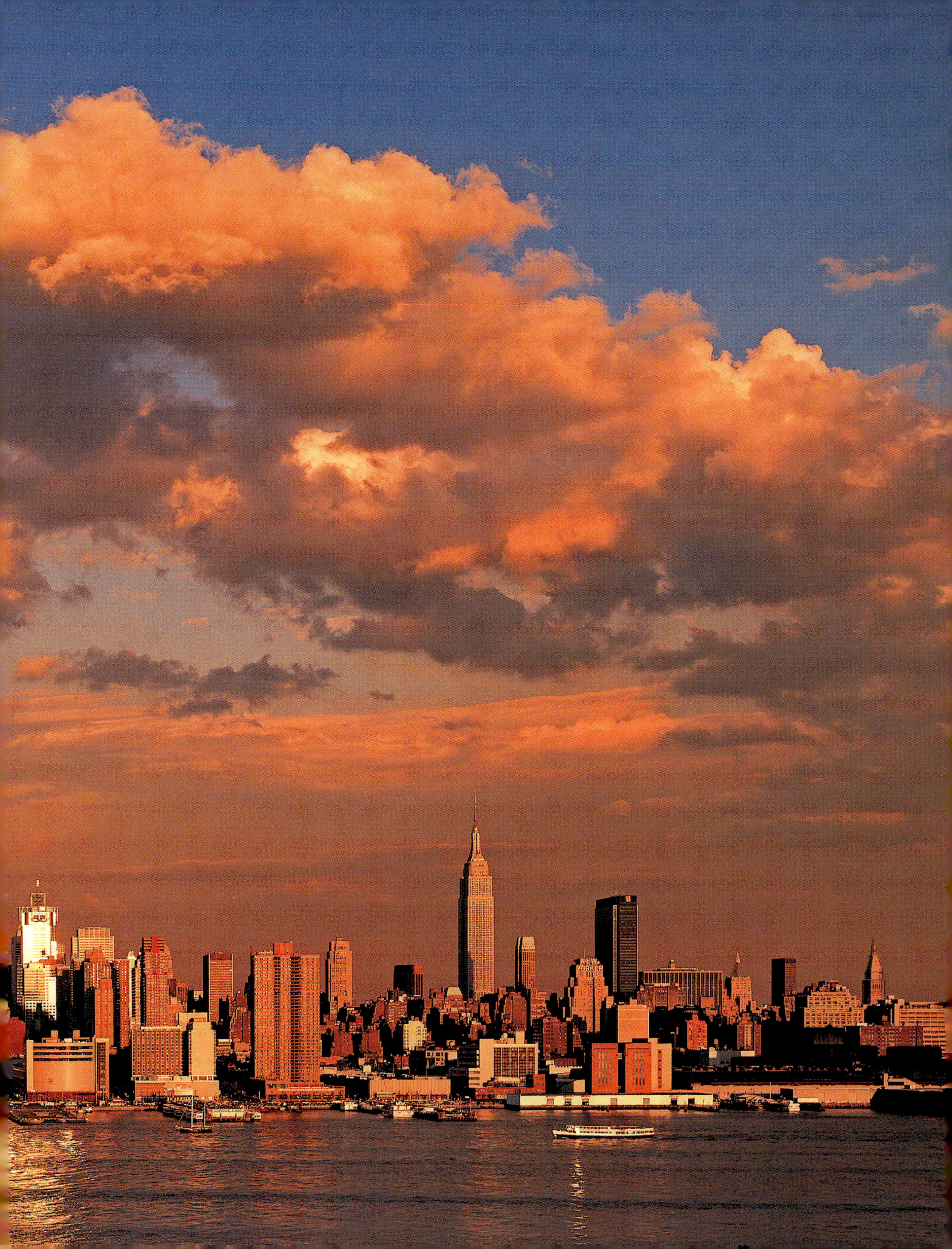
NEW
YORKER

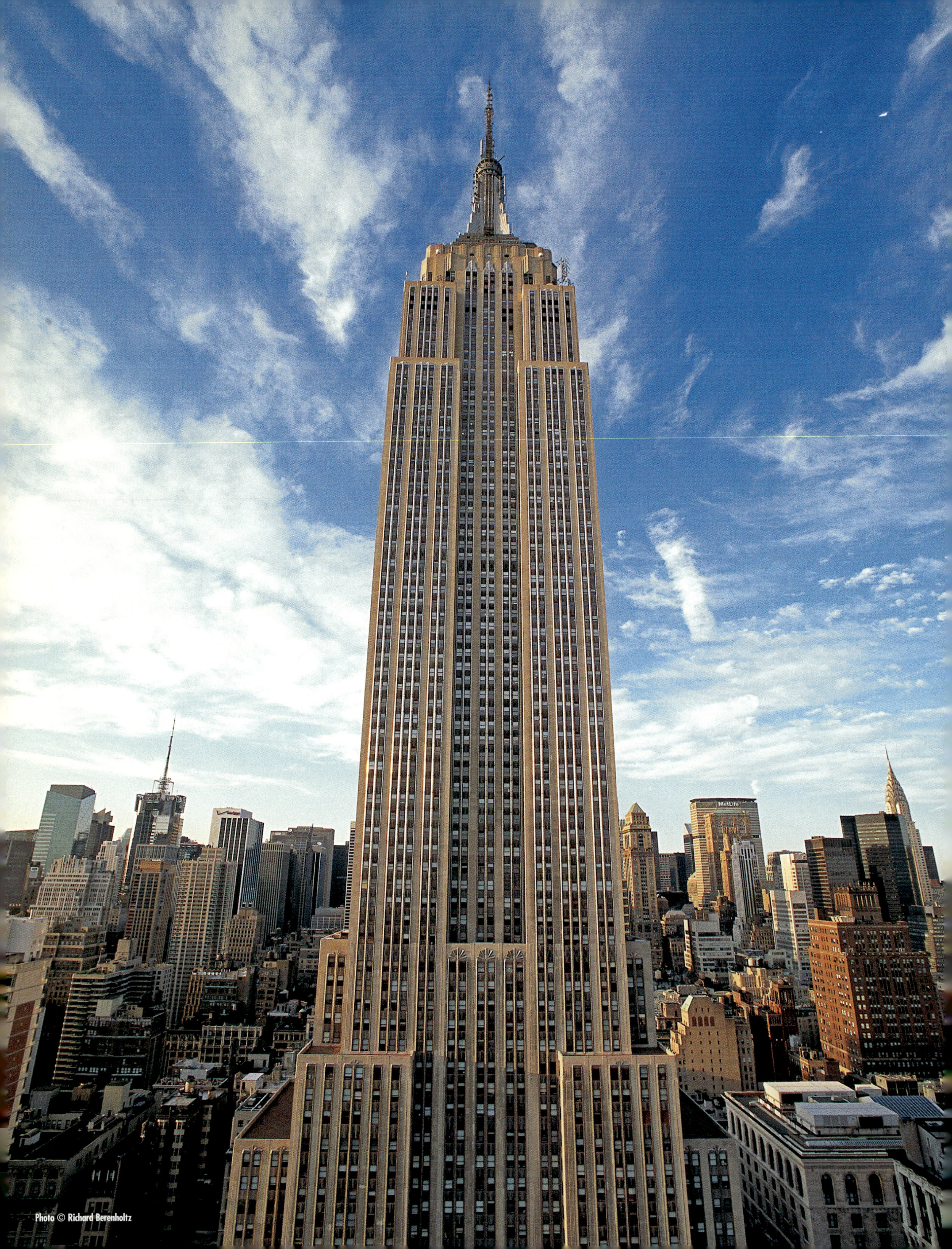

Photo © Richard Berenholtz